The Metaverse Investing: Complete Beginners' Guide to Digital Asset

A Starter Guide and Basic Concepts about Metaverse and The Digital World for Beginners to Learn from Scratch

By

Koala Publishers

Charles Murphy

Disclaimer Notice

This book is written and published independently. Please keep in mind that the material in this publication is solely for educational and entertaining purposes. All efforts have provided authentic, up-to-date, trustworthy, and comprehensive information. There are no express or implied assurances. The purpose of this book's material is to assist readers in having a better understanding of the subject matter. The activities, information, and exercises are provided solely for self-help information. This book is not intended to replace expert psychologists, legal, financial, or other guidance. If you require counseling, please get in touch with a qualified professional.

By reading this text, the reader accepts that the author will not be held liable for any damages, indirectly or directly, experienced due to the use of the information included herein, particularly, but not limited to, omissions, errors, or inaccuracies. As a reader, you are accountable for your decisions, actions, and consequences.

About the Author

Charles Murphy is a Professor in Computer Science and Technology by profession. He has an eye for future technological trends as he is always eager to learn new things and share them with the audience. He has shown keen interest in the newest technological fields like Metaverse and Non-Fungible Tokens (NFTs) He is already investing in NFTs and coming up with his books to help the readers as much as possible. The best thing is that he always maintains the level of practicality in his books so that the readers come up with positive feedback after getting maximum learning. Along with a book on Metaverse Investment, he has also written a book on the value of NFTs and how they can be of any help for those who want to get greater profits in the said fields. He wants to share his expertise and deep knowledge with the readers so that they also jump into such a technological domain for earning profits.

Table of contents

Introduction

The notion of a metaverse has existed for some time and it is gathering attention all over the world. Once the Metaverse is fully understood, this situation is easily adaptable to our Sunday afternoon activities.

You may have heard about Facebook's rebranding as Meta Platforms and its eventual goal of integrating a Metaverse into daily life (Zuckerberg's Interview). Make no mistake if you are unfamiliar with the Metaverse. Is Virtual Reality (VR) a toy, a fad, or a monstrous advertising universe? It is a mixture of everything and nothing. I will define the Metaverse and discuss what it can accomplish for you.

Today's exploration of the Metaverse is a bigger notion. The concept is to enter cyberspace using virtual reality glasses and interact with the world totally as if it were genuine.

Without further ado, let us define the Metaverse.

First, a virtual environment is referred to as the "Metaverse." There is more than one Metaverse; there are several. Sports, films, artwork, casinos, exploration, construction, purchasing, selling, and conversing are all possible within any metaverse. Assume that the Metaverse is a virtual universe. Within that digital world, you interact with everything the Metaverse has to offer. You must have certainly heard the term "metaverse" a lot over time; it often refers to a computer-generated cosmos that exists independently of science fiction books. At times, the line between a "metaverse" and a reasonably interactive virtual reality environment can get blurred. Many people feel this is only a marketing gimmick, and Facebook's recent rebranding of its controlling shareholder to "Meta" has fueled this belief. This perspective, however, may be erroneous. Numerous metaverse-like properties can be discovered in common objects. Consider home heating systems: they are primarily software-controlled, but we have far more control over our heating by using several physical sensors and, expectedly, a physical interface that displays the system's condition.

To simplify the process, the software representation of the system may be equivalent to the physical configuration. Our entire homes would be virtualized on a metaverse platform in the future. This would encompass home heating, security, and entertainment systems, as well as intelligent appliances such as refrigerators and washers. What is the purpose? It is not as if I need to wander around my house in 3D to turn off a heater. Due to metaverses, it may be possible to play games with family and friends from across the nation. How about streaming services such as Netflix, Hulu, and others? It would be fun to reunite with old friends and see a movie together in the Metaverse. Here's what you will learn about Metaverse and how to profit from it as a non-traditional investor, as well as why investing in Metaverse makes sense!

Catchphrases come and go in the world of technology. Nevertheless, a few of them persist. Artificial intelligence, augmented reality, virtual reality, cryptocurrency, and blockchain — the list goes on and on as technology progresses and develops at a breakneck pace.

Consider doing business meetings and interviews through a virtual office rather than through zoom or webcam. Consider putting on garments in the convenience of your own home — the next great thing in teleportation and Metanomics.

The Metaverse is a newly coined concept that is here to stay. The Metaverse, which mixes multiple technical components such as virtual reality, augmented reality, and video, allows users to "live" in a digital universe. The Metaverse's proponents see its users working, playing, and interacting with friends via anything from concerts and seminars to virtual work trips.

The Metaverse has no one creator or definition. It is approximately equivalent to the World Wide Web in terms of the digital environment, but users may engage digitally through social networking, augmented reality, online gaming, and cryptocurrency.

The Metaverse exists as an extension of the physical universe, a three-dimensional environment with which individuals may penetrate and interact. It will probably become the most popular venue globally, but it will almost surely not start flawlessly. Comprehensive virtual reality will take time to grow into a completely digitalized environment. Neal Stephenson coined the term "Metaverse" in 1992 with his novel "Snow Crash."

The Metaverse may be a decentralized system where individuals may produce and exchange works regardless of their content or format.

Numerous breakthroughs since then have paved the way for the creation of a true metaverse, an online digital realm that mixes virtual reality, augmented reality, 3D holographic avatars, video, and other modes of communication.

For some time, Facebook has been investigating virtual and immersive technologies for the Metaverse. Additionally, CEO Mark Zuckerberg has stated that he expects the social media company would one day be dubbed a "metaverse corporation." Facebook unveiled a large metaverse campaign in Europe this week, reiterating the concept. There are presently indications of the Metaverse in online game worlds such as Fortnite, Minecraft, and Roblox.

In a July interview with the technology website The Verge, Mark Zuckerberg stated that he was making a distinction between the Metaverse idea and the standard "two-dimensional" webpages that today dominate the internet.

Numerous forms of the Metaverse have existed for a long period, whether in the realms of social media, augmented reality, online gaming, or cryptocurrency.

Second Life, Fortnite, Minecraft, and Roblox are examples of collaborative and world-building games that use Metaverse-related gameplay elements. Users may work and engage with one another, attend events, and real-world exchange currency for digital goods and services in the virtual marketplace.

However, these universes have mostly stayed separated from one another. Metaverse enthusiasts envision a virtual cosmos in which individuals may seamlessly switch between these many types of virtual reality. Users may even preserve the same assumed identity from the world to the universe — via a virtual avatar — and whatever money they collect in one universe will be worth the same in the other. Everybody will be able to pay using internationally recognized digital money.

Despite the term's ambiguity, proponents believe that the Metaverse will eventually be a 3D world that overlays the real world, where individuals will be able to purchase, play games, and transact in collaborative virtual spaces.

Assume you, like Mark Zuckerberg, believe in the Metaverse. In that scenario, it is "an embodied internet that you are a part of," where "creation, avatars, and digital objects" are necessary for self-expression and result in "whole new experiences and economic opportunities."

This book will go extensively into the Metaverse. We will cover a variety of topics, including technology, philosophy, and economics, to guarantee that you have the knowledge necessary to participate in this revolution. This book covers the fundamentals of the Metaverse, as well as its link to your health and well-being.

The Milestones of Metaverse

What is now occurring that may pave the way for the future Metaverse is as follows:

Meta

The digital behemoth, once known as Facebook, has already made many significant investments in augmented worlds, including the acquisition of Oculus in 2014. Meta envisions a virtual world where virtual reality headset-wearing digital avatars interact for jobs, travel, and recreation. Zuckerberg is bullish on the Metaverse, believing that it can supplant the conventional computer. Mark Zuckerberg, CEO of Meta, stated that the "next platform and media would be considerably more extensive and will embody the internet where you are, not just gazing at it." "We refer to this as the metaverse."

Microsoft

Using its Microsoft Mesh platform, the software behemoth already uses holograms and focuses on mixed or extended reality (XR) programs that combine reality with virtual and augmented reality. Microsoft showcased its aspirations to introduce mixed reality capabilities to Microsoft Teams by 2022, including holographic pictures and virtual avatars. Additionally, explorable 3D virtual interconnected retail and workplace spaces are being developed for deployment. The United States Army is developing the HoloLens 2 augmented reality headgear for troops to train, rehearse and combat in conjunction with Microsoft. Additionally, Xbox Live connects millions of video gamers from across the world through its online service.

Epic Games

The platform, which launched in 2004, features a slew of user-generated games, including role-playing games such as Bloxburg and Brookhaven, in which players create houses, go to work, and act out scenarios. Roblox is now valued at significantly more than $45 billion following its first public offering. On the day of the platform's initial public offering (IPO) in March, inventor and CEO David Baszucki sent out a thank-you tweet, thanking everyone who had helped to bring the site "another step closer to fulfilling our dream of the # Metaverse." As a result, Roblox has partnered with roller skating shoe company Vans to create Vans World, a simulated roller skating park where users can dress up in new Vans gear, and a limited-edition Gucci Garden, where participants can try on and purchase apparel for their virtual selves. Additionally, Roblox has partnered with several other brands, like Vans and Gucci.

Minecraft

Minecraft, which is owned by Microsoft and is another virtual world popular with children, is the digital equivalent of Legos in that players can customize their digital avatar and build anything they want in the game. Since August, the business claims that Minecraft has had over 140 million monthly active users. The virus has exploded in popularity among children who rely heavily on virtual connections.

On the internet, several lesser-known enterprises have built their virtual worlds. Second life, a 2003-founded online fantasy world, is already in its second decade as an alternate reality.

The internet's secure haven: There are no permanent or temporary virtual locations (for public or private use) where concerts, fairs, reunions, and conferences may be held the same way as they are in the virtual world. The Windmill Factory, a New York-based production company that began working on the service, collaborated with Lady Gaga and Nine Inch Nails.

The Sensorium Galaxy, which debuted its first two connected online "worlds" in 2021, is a projected galaxy of numerous connected online "worlds" that can be explored via virtual reality headsets or desktop computers. When it comes to music, Prism, the first to open, has virtual DJs and bands that play in futuristic environs.

Chapter 1: Metaverse

We shall explore metaverse currencies, tokens, and wallets, as well as blockchain metaverse businesses, crypto-metaverse initiatives, and the Metaverse's general functioning, in this book.

A "metaverse" is an immersive virtual environment in which players, often represented by avatars, interact with one another, construct in-world objects and landscapes, and create experiences.

1.1 The Concept of Metaverse Investing

A crypto metaverse is a virtual environment in which blockchain technology serves as the foundation for an economy based on crypto-assets such as metaverse tokens. Numerous metaverse tokens are frequently used to represent crypto assets and things like digital land and products in the Metaverse. The ownership history of each currency is kept on the blockchain, and they may be traded for digital assets such as bitcoin (BTC) and Ether (ETH) through a variety of decentralized exchange platforms (DEXs).

A recent study indicates that the physical world gradually merges with the Metaverse.

Numerous firms, both mainstream and crypto-native, have established virtual offices in crypto metaverses where they host virtual events and festivals that attract thousands of monthly visitors and generate millions of dollars in revenue.

For instance, in the blockchain game Decentral, the renowned auction firm Sotheby's created a digital duplicate of its London headquarters in 2021 that will be accessible to the public. At the venue, Metaverse users will explore a multi-room virtual art display. Decentral conducts monthly live music concerts, talks, and meetings along with its other activities.

1.2 The Metaverse's Cryptography Field Guide

Verifiable and immutable ownership of digital objects and money will be necessary for the Metaverse. No longer is the phrase "metaverse" reserved for science fiction. When technology affects our lives, it is unsurprising. To mention a few inventions, the internet, the smartphone, and the cloud all had their debuts in science fiction before finding their way into the real world. The next big thing in the digital era is almost certainly on the horizon, and it has the potential to transform how we live our everyday lives profoundly. The term "metaverse" is used to refer to this phenomenon.

The Metaverse is a single location that combines virtual reality, augmented reality, and the internet. You can see how it presents itself in popular video games such as Roblox, Fortnite, and Animal Crossing. The word was coined in Neal Stephenson's 1992 science fiction novel Snow Crash. The story follows a couple of delivery couriers as they traverse the Metaverse to seek a way out of a capitalist dystopia.
Numerous futurists envisage a metaverse akin to those shown in science fiction films such as Ready Player One, in which

individuals may interact. Essentially, users would be able to move seamlessly between locations with thousands of other people, all within the same digital domain, much like they would at a limitless virtual theme park.

1.3 Exploring the Metaverse is both enjoyable and educational

Fortnite, Roblox, and Second Life demonstrate the most remarkable links between modern games and the Metaverse. When the Metaverse is completely functioning, it will be several orders of magnitude larger than it is now. After the Metaverse is fully formed, it will consist of three critical components:

The importance of interoperability, presence and standardization cannot be overstated.

According to forecasts, humans will soon communicate electronically and travel between virtual environments via avatars and other digital goods. Payments made with cryptocurrencies such as bitcoin (BTC) and Ethereum (ETH) will almost certainly supplant fiat money in the future.

The Metaverse is projected to have a major effect on virtually every business while also creating a plethora of new economic opportunities. As a result, it may become a popular location for investors.

1.4 What Is the Metaverse's Importance?

Even if the Metaverse falls short of many people's extravagant expectations, it has the potential to transform our relationships with the digital world significantly. As non-fungible tokens (NFT) did for producers, gamers, and artists, a collaborative virtual experience can do the same for the creative economy, restructuring it and creating it.

The Metaverse's virtual environment has the potential to become a trillion-dollar industry unto itself. Some individuals utilize it as a place of work, while others use it as a shopping and leisure destination. The Metaverse is referred to as the internet's replacement, not as an extension of it. Entrepreneur and author Matthew Ball believe it will act as a catalyst for the emergence of a new generation of enterprises, just like the internet did. As seen, the rise of digital platforms can destabilize existing market leaders. This is one of the most exciting features.

1.5 Two of the most prominent social media platforms are Facebook and the Metaverse.

Mark Zuckerberg informed Facebook staff at the end of June that he would be bringing the Metaverse into life. The company has created a team of experts to oversee the initiative, including Vishal Shah and Vivek Sharma of Instagram and Jason Rubin of Facebook Gaming, and other individuals.

In an interview with The Verge, Zuckerberg described his idea for the Metaverse as follows: "Infinity offices" or "virtual workplaces" were his notions. He argues that working in virtual reality enables better multitasking and that working in a virtual, metaverse-like environment is fundamentally more productive and collaborative. Zoom chats have clear limits, and Zuckerberg has stated that he prefers virtual reality meetings when feasible.

He also explored the possibility of the Metaverse assisting in correcting socioeconomic injustices. According to Raj Chetty's research, Zuckerberg thinks that a person's geographic location has a substantial influence on their financial potential. However, in a future where the Metaverse is extensively used, this concept is partially reversed, with remote work becoming more accessible as virtual and augmented reality technology progresses, as is now the case.

Facebook intends to be the driving force behind this growth through its investments. It currently controls Oculus, a company best known for developing the popular Quest virtual reality headset. While virtual reality technology is still in its infancy, Zuckerberg believes that it will be ready for metaverse capabilities by the end of the decade, if not sooner.

1.6 The tech titans are investigating the Metaverse.

Other technology titans are also making inroads into the Metaverse. Although no one individual or business has power over the Metaverse, the typical suspects in the information technology sector have already asserted influence over the space's destiny. In several ways, gaming is light years ahead of other metaverse technologies, and it has the potential to establish the industry standard in the years to come. The concept of in-game economies has played a significant role throughout the history of video games.

Players can acquire and exchange items that have no real worth outside of the game's setting through in-game economies. Fortnite is the most recent video game, but other examples include the continued success of titles such as Grand Theft Auto V.

As a strong online community remains engaged with the game's online, open-world setting, the game generated more than a billion dollars in profit in 2020. The developers claim that our interaction with it will be more akin to connecting to the internet than with a virtual role-playing game.

According to Michael Gord, co-founder of the Metaverse Group, those who remain skeptical could examine the patterns created by the epidemic. The Metaverse Group is a real estate investment trust focused on developing a portfolio of assets in Decentral and other worlds such as Somnium Space, Sandbox, and Upland. The Metaverse Group, headquartered in Decentral, is a real estate investment trust manager. According to Mr. Gord, "investors have a popular conviction that gold is concealed beneath those pixelated hills. Consider visiting New York when it was still countryside and having the option of a SoHo property or a block in Central Park," he added. If someone wants to purchase a piece of SoHo real estate at the moment, it is a gold mine since it is not on the market. The Metaverse will see the identical event that occurred on Earth.

Tokens.com was also successful in arranging a larger property acquisition for roughly $2 million in Decentral and the fashion area. This was the largest real estate transaction in metaverse history, according to the company. The property would be transformed into a virtual commerce center for high-end designer companies equivalent to Rodeo Drive or Fifth Avenue. According to him, his metaverse portfolio is worth up to ten times what he paid for it, and much of his reasoning will be recognizable to anybody who has ever purchased or sold real estate in the real world.

According to him, it is all about location, location, location. When it comes to real estate, a piece of land in an urban center that receives high tourist traffic is more valuable than land in the suburbs. Scarcity has a monetary value. Many of these digital universes assume the reality of cartoonish, gummy-colored dreamlands, while others are digital extensions of familiar and beloved realities, such as the world of video games. Owners may buy pieces of land for emotional or economic reasons. However, once they own the NFT, they are entitled to a part of any commerce conducted on that piece of property. And when the Metaverse grows more prevalent in our everyday experience, a new domain emerges in which the distinction between the two is lost: the omniverse (universe without end).

According to Justin Bannon, co-founder and CEO of Boson Protocol, which enables the sale of non-fungible tokens (NFTs) representing actual objects in the Metaverse, the real world and the online world are merging into a single hybrid reality in which the fungible and non-fungible coexist at various points in time. The commerce that enables this change will be housed in metaverse real estate. He stated that it is already occurring; it is only a matter of degree. However, I believe that in five years, my daughter will refuse to allow me to pick her up from school unless I am wearing footwear that features a non-marking sole.

In June, boson Protocol purchased a large block of land in the Decentral and Vegas City casino zones. According to the company, the region would be transformed into a commerce hub for exchanging physical goods for NFTs. The same NFTs, which work as digital representations of physical things, will be traded in traditional retail facilities for commodities. Everybody recognizes that we are still in the early stages of the game and that these artifacts will be regarded as modern-day antiquities. Thus, purchasing at this point is highly profitable.

There are just a few digital platforms where investors may purchase and sell real estate, and each one operates on its own business. Mana, for example, is the money of Decentraland. Additionally, Decentraland provides a marketplace for non-financial assets (NFTs), such as land parcels for sale. Mr. Kiguel likened it to a multiple listing service (MLS). Rather than hosting the events in a digital stadium, Wave, an entertainment company that produces interactive concerts such as Mr. Bieber's, generates revenue by selling virtual merchandise and securing brand sponsorships for the events, which take place in neutral zones rather than digital stadiums. Although the company has not yet monetized real estate, co-founder and CEO Adam Arrigo has indicated that he is investigating the prospect.

He noted in his presentation that platforms such as Decentraland and Sandbox are pioneering to verify these bits of property, these stores. Over the next few years, our work will get significantly greater recognition and acceptance.

1.7 What do you propose to do with the Metaverse territory?

Fortune magazine published a story recently about an architectural business that assists customers in creating new land tracts. What should you do with a piece of digital property once you own it? This is a new question that has come up after the real estate deals. One company, Voxel Architects, has done a great job of changing this business. Voxel Architects has built more than 40 digital structures for clients like Sotheby's auction house and ConsenSys Software, the creator of the popular cryptocurrency wallet Meta Mask.

Additionally, business is brisk. There were about ten requests for design estimates every week. Now, almost 30 people ask for them every week, says George Bileca, Voxel Architects' chief design officer; this is a big change.

According to Leandro Bellone, CEO of NFT Studios, the cost of a project can range between $10,000 and $300,000, depending on the scope and complexity of the project, the number of capabilities integrated, and the time required to complete the construction. You can also build in most of these virtual worlds using the platform's native building software. While building structures in the Sandbox is possible via the game creator, building structures on land controlled by you is possible via the in-game constructor in Decentraland.

Snoop Dogg, who is currently working on the Snoop verse for the Sandbox, has sold the rights to be his virtual next-door neighbor to a company called Sandbox for $450,000.

1.8 What is the optimal method of payment for metaverse real estate?

To become a landowner, you must first become acquainted with the bitcoin market.

- **How to Invest in Metaverse Digital Real Estate?**

You must first create a cryptocurrency wallet before acquiring land. After downloading Meta Mask (or another type of crypto wallet), you will be prompted to create a password. Additionally, you will very certainly be given a secret word that will be used to verify your identity at a later time. You can use your newly generated crypto wallet to create a Decentraland or sandbox account if you want. Also, keep in mind that you should do a lot of research on any metaverse platform before investing in it.

After you get a cryptocurrency wallet, you will need to change your US dollars into the cryptocurrency of your choice. Your debit or credit card can be used in conjunction with the Meta Mask Google Chrome plugin so that you can quickly get Ether, which is the most common cryptocurrency used for land transactions. Wire or Transak are two places where you can buy and sell cryptocurrency. When you are ready to finish your transaction, Meta Mask will send you there. It is essential to keep in mind that both Wire and Transak charge a fee to convert US dollars to Ether (or other types of cryptocurrencies).

There are various brokers and specialists available to assist you in selecting where to acquire land, including NFT Property Group, MetaMetrics Solutions, and the Metaverse Group. WeMeta is another website that can assist you in scouting potential residences.

1.9 Acquiring real estate is a possibility in the Metaverse.

Engineers say that the Metaverse will be fully functioning as an economy in a few years, giving us an asynchronous digital experience on par with email and social networking now, if not even before.

Because the blockchain facilitates finance in the Metaverse, money is represented in these digital worlds by a cryptocurrency. A blockchain is a decentralized record of transactions that eliminates the need for a trusted third party, such as a bank. The NFT is used to establish ownership and cannot be used with other types of documents or identities.

The speed and volume of commercial real estate transactions in the Metaverse have increased in the last few months.

In October 2021, Tokens.com, a blockchain technology company specializing in non-fungible tokens (NFTs) and metaverse real estate, acquired a 50% share in Metaverse Group, one of the world's first virtual real estate enterprises, for around $1.7 million. While Metaverse Group's headquarters are in Toronto, its virtual offices are located in Decentraland in Crypto Valley, the Metaverse's Silicon Valley. Additionally, Decentraland has gaming, commerce, fashion, and arts industries.

Tokens.com has now officially broken ground, although digitally, on a tower in Decentraland. Tokens.com has already welcomed high-end brands like Louis Vuitton, Gucci, and Burberry into the Metaverse through NFTs. This gives business leaders hope that the Tokens.com tower will soon be making money from leasing and advertising for these brands.

1.10 Cryptocurrency is critical in the Metaverse.

Permissionless identification, financial services, and high-speed commerce will be necessary inside and outside the Metaverse. Data must be gathered, stored, and distributed globally to millions, if not billions, of individuals. Bitcoin's technology has the answer to overcoming these issues.

Mana is Decentraland's native currency, and it can be acquired on cryptocurrency exchanges like Coinbase and Bittrex.

Indeed, there are casinos in Decentraland where you may place bets in MANA and where dealers are reimbursed in MANA for turning up to work.

The highest transaction to date, at almost $900,000, was a non-traditional transaction (NFT) for a 259-parcel virtual estate in Decentraland. Users will be able to purchase and sell virtual products from various games and planets once interoperable markets are developed. NFTs could be used to represent all virtual goods and things that aren't tangible. Cryptocurrencies could one day replace fiat money as the only legal way to pay in the Metaverse.

Many people are taken aback by how much money gamers invest in digital products, and I believe this is true. Converting such assets to NFTs and building an NFT economy will benefit the current digital economy by adding a new layer. While no one can anticipate precisely how the Metaverse will appear or when it will arrive in its ultimate form, one thing is certain: cryptocurrencies will play a crucial part in its development. As we observe the expansion of technologies such as virtual reality and the increasing involvement of established industry titans like Facebook, it is evident that improvements in blockchain technology and the cryptocurrency sector will play an equal part in determining Metaverse's future.

Chapter 2: Web 3.0

Web 3 does not refer to a single program but to a collection of cryptocurrency-backed initiatives that collaborate to establish an ecosystem of decentralized internet services. What services, then? It may be anything from decentralized social media to having an open forum where individuals can openly argue and express themselves rather than news controlled by a single organization. Users have control and privacy over their data when it is decentralized. How? by utilizing cryptocurrency and blockchain technology. It liberates consumers from relying on any government or organization to accomplish their goals.

Before we get into the inner workings of Web 3, it is necessary to review the history of Web 1.0. Websites played a similar function to conventional media in the 1990s, the dot.com era when content was one-sided, and consumers could consume it. Like how print newspapers charge for advertisements, websites like Yahoo charge to appear at the top of the search results regardless of how many people click on the link.

Then, as social media grew in popularity, web two was developed, and the emphasis shifted to trending, popular content generated by other people. Although the border between consumers and creators of content was blurred, Web 2 introduced a slew of complications. The most notable of these are concerns about censorship and privacy. Google, Facebook, and Twitter actively stifle any dialogue contradicting their narrative. Donald Trump was barred from social media, so what chance do you have if an active US president and billionaire cannot speak freely? Web 3 refers to the internet's design, enabling users to be independent of any one organization or government, allowing them to do anything they choose.

2.1 A Brief history

Tim Berners-Lee created the "web" as we know it in Switzerland in the early 1990s. Internet browsers would not be available until almost a half-decade later. Some years later, search engines such as Google were created. Since that time, the web and internet technology has evolved dramatically. Nowadays, internet use has evolved into a means of survival for millions. The internet's history has been divided into three distinct eras.

The Static Web - Web 1.0

At first, the internet's content was predefined. As a result, the phrase "static web" was coined to characterize it. Static content is defined as any content that may be supplied to an end-user without being created, updated, or processed. You could create a website and allow visitors to peruse it, but they would be unable to interact with it other than leaving a comment.

The primary distinction between mainstream media and Web 1.0 is how users participate in content consumption. The internet has irreversibly altered our lives by decentralizing content production. Until the internet, only a few media sources generated and disseminated information. Access to the internet enables everyone to create content. Additionally, consumers may influence content development by ignoring material they dislike. As a result, Web 1.0 is sometimes referred to as the "democratization of information."

It is critical to understand the decentralization of content production. This thinking eventually resulted in currency decentralization and the birth of new technologies such as Bitcoin. In other words, if you intend to do anything in the Metaverse, remember that this internet principle always determines online company success.

The Interactive Web - Web 2.0

The internet's democratization and decentralization eventually resulted in Web 2.0. People were not confined to absorbing content or leaving their two cents in the comment area during this era. They may become content providers as a result of Web 2.0. Wikipedia, YouTube, WordPress, and Blogger illustrate Web 2.0's global reach.

With the "dot-com bubble," Web 2.0 got off to a rocky start. The dot-com bubble was a fast rise in the prices of US technology stocks in the late 1990s, fueled by investments in Web-based businesses. The bubble burst in 2001, resulting in a 77 percent drop in the Nasdaq and investor fear. Numerous web firms went bankrupt, and for a brief while, it appeared as though the web was a passing craze.

This was not the case. Technology was progressing and increasing at a healthy clip. The issue was with the stock markets. A wonderful example of this is Jeff Bezos of Amazon.

Even though Amazon lost 90% of its value during the bubble, it made its stockholders enormously wealthy, including Bezos, one of the world's wealthiest individuals. If such a scenario develops in the metaverse age, one thing to remember is that long-term investors will always win out as long as technology advances.

As a result of Web 2.0, the internet has become a sea of user-generated content. The practice of sharing knowledge and engaging with people has become well established. It resulted in the establishment of hundreds of thousands of online stores, content production platforms, and the emergence of the influencer age.

The Semantic Web - Web 3.0

Web 3.0 is expected to be dubbed the Semantic Web due to its increased intuitiveness for all users. The term was invented by Tim Berners-Lee, the Founder of the World Wide Web. In 2001, the journal Scientific American published an essay in which Bernes-Lee detailed his vision for the internet. As an illustration, he demonstrated two brothers who coordinate logistics for their mother's medical care, utilizing intelligent agents. They automate the process by connecting with clinical systems, one another, and their home equipment.

This is the type of intuitive technology that Web 3.0 will provide. The purpose of the third generation of the web is to give users an experience tailored to their interests and requirements. Alexa, a service provided by Amazon that gathers information from the web and tailors it to our specific requirements, is a classic example of Web 3.0 technology.

We are now in the process of migrating from Web 2.0 to Web 3.0. Web 3.0 is expected to have the same magnitude of influence as Web 2.0. Web 3.0 will usher in a slew of novel technologies, including the Metaverse.

This section will discuss some of the fundamental components of Web 3 and some of the space leaders. These fundamental components range from domain name registry to cloud data storage and processing and are collectively referred to as smart contract platforms in the crypto world.

2.2 Domain Name Registry

When you visit a website, such as google.com, the portion preceding the dot is the subdomain, which is Google. The section after the dot, which is.com, is the top-level domain. The top-level domain leases the domain. As a result, VeriSign, which controls the top-level domain dot com, rents it to Google. A dot com or dot net domain is never yours to own.

In comparison to Web 3, it is a public marketplace where people may bid on their top-level domains. For instance, the handshake is a market leader in this space. Their HNS token implements a vickery-style auction, enabling users to acquire and rent whatever domain they like.

That is a pretty quick explanation, but let us move on to the next web3 component, cloud data storage.

2.3 Cloud Data Storage

Widely known, Amazon and Google are the market leaders in web-based cloud storage. However, on Web 3, several rivals avoid censorship and do not snoop on their consumers. Filecoin, Siacoin, and Arweave are just a few competitors, but there are many more. Peer-to-peer data sharing is facilitated, and individuals are rewarded for hosting and receiving payment in the project's native coin.

Either data is directly kept on the blockchain, or the blockchain is used to monitor payments to the data host. For instance, Siacoin divides data into categories and requires servers to collateral. If the host defaults on their payment before the end of their paid hosting term, they forfeit their collateral, motivating them to guarantee no data is lost. Additionally, there are several duplicate hosts for each of the various groups.

Arweave takes another approach. Arweave inserts any data that has ever been processed. When hosts want miners to update new data, referred to as a "block of data," they must demonstrate that all previous data is included. This has the advantage of establishing a permanent record that is highly valuable for non-censored historical recordkeeping.

Web 3's final component is computer processing, which in cryptocurrency is referred to as a "Smart Contract platform." With Web 2, data is processed on the computer or network of a single business. However, they can modify the rules and either filter or prohibit people.

On the other hand, Web 3 processes data on the blockchain, making it permissionless and censorship-resistant. The code is referred to as a "contract" because it represents an agreement between two parties to process data on the blockchain. At present, Ethereum, Polkadot, Cardano, and even ICP, or internet computers, are among the market leaders in this space, integrating a decentralized cloud with a smart contract platform.

These are the fundamentals of Web 3, and you may purchase all of the tokens covered here, as well as many more planned projects. While this is the bare-bones architecture for how Web 3 will function, the possibilities for what people will accomplish with their newly acquired freedom of speech are unlimited.

Chapter 3: Owning Digital Assets and Principles of Metanomics

Metanomics is the study of economic regulation and business principles in the Metaverse. Additionally, it examines how real-world businesses might incorporate virtual worlds into their larger strategy. Further, Metanomics involves using virtual worlds as research laboratories for real-world businesses and policy concerns.

You may be in a Metaverse right now and are unaware of it. Digital objects are frequently acquired for the same reasons physical items are. Indeed, there is a sense of belonging to unique subgroups or organizations and speculation and possible advantages.

3.1 The Distinctive Traits of Metaverse

Virtual apparel, avatar cosmetics, digital property investment, residences, and automobiles will be valued in the Metaverse. The Netvrk, one of the most prominent cryptocurrency Metaverse companies, recently had a car sale that sold out rapidly. There are no limits to what you can do in the Metaverse if you create outstanding content and promote it well since NFT's popularity shows no signs of decreasing.

Virtual careers would be regarded in the Metonymy. Metaverse advisors, virtual real estate developers, automotive and land leasing, and avatar architects, to name a few. Businesses will need to pivot away from online guidance and a shared virtual economy. As an example of a project, Envoy comes to mind. Consider a decentralized advertising panel, such as the one in Times Square in New York.

According to some, Metanomics acts as an asymmetrical buffer against actual events, and Metonymy has the potential to become the greatest form of capitalism, driven entirely by free-market forces inside the Meta- community. Additionally, for those seeking to store their money, the convenience of holding assets across borders may be immensely enticing.

Let us examine this more closely. People will visit brands in the Metaverse out of a sense of connection, not because of a need for a product or service.
When making an organic sale, you must enable your customers to immerse themselves in the experience.

Consider the following excellent examples: Travis Scott raked about $20 million in garment sales in less than a week. This is down from the 1.7 million recordings he made in a single night during his in-person Astroworld tour and slightly less than 40% of the 53.5 million visits he chronicled. Nevertheless, artists with a smaller fan following may hold virtual world events to increase digital record sales, streaming, and commemorative digital products.

Yes, the ten-year-old notion of a concert t-shirt may now be transformed into an NFT or game skin. You previously played games for entertainment and leisure, but now is the time to invest and begin earning money.

We will take the risk of projecting that the newer generation of tech-savvy kids would reject the old educational system and normal student jobs in favor of earning a wonderful profession and enjoying it in the Metaverse.

At the World Economic Forum, one speaker explained why most jobs can now be automated and how a useless class of humanity will develop. While one economic sector closes its doors to the average worker, another expands with new options and possibilities, enabling AI and the web to thrive.

There are now social media ramifications of artificial intelligence (AI). Now, artificial intelligence would be employed to develop, populate, and sustain the Metaverse. Instruments such as AI that learns and identifies viewers may hold the key to the Metaverse being the game industry's next frontier.

Additionally, AI will play a part in the Metaverse by learning about you over time and tailoring your Metaverse experience to your tastes. The Founder of a virtual influencer agency leverages artificial intelligence and social listening to create the optimal match between personalities, speaking styles, and the target audience. These predictions may also alter the player's experience with the most engaging information and interactions.

From creating digital environments to shaping more realistic AI character behaviors to automating bug identification, you may envision an AI system curating or creating content and experiences according to your preferences. The applications of artificial intelligence will be practically limitless. We are hopeful about the Metaverse, regardless of its eventual form.

Artificial intelligence would be necessary for the successful completion of large-scale initiatives. Web 3.0 has far greater capacity and compatibility than any prior service. Remote work, teleconferencing, telemedicine, and remote socializing, among a variety of other possibilities, have been significantly extended. It is reasonable to anticipate that the Metaverse will become a significant element of the everyday lives of ordinary people during the next decade and beyond.

This has several repercussions, including Metapolitics. This adds dimension to social paradigms. Social movements and trends can permeate the physical world and vice versa.

One day, just as we need a single network technology to run websites and everything else, we will require a single global blockchain. Interoperability and all those disparate old currencies look to be more of a hindrance than a help when having a nice experience.

There is currently a notion referred to as a meta-network. It has been in use for years and is built on the same technology as the original bitcoin. It is currently traded under the symbol BSV, which the crypto community has been socially engineered to loathe.

We believe that a unified global blockchain will be necessary. At the moment, BSV is the only blockchain capable of withstanding this kind of commercial pressure or usage. According to Satoshi Nakamoto, the current Visa credit card network facilitates over 15 million Internet sales worldwide. Bitcoin already scales far more than conventional technology at a fraction of the cost. It never reaches the scale's maximum capacity. According to Moore's law, hardware will double in speed every five years and triple in speed every ten years.

Even if Bitcoin's popularity increases exponentially, we expect computing capabilities to continue to surpass transaction volume. People are still attempting to construct a faster blockchain. According to Satoshi Nakamoto, the most advanced blockchain to date is bitcoin. In a private email to Mike Han about this knowledge.

3.2 Exploring the Inner Workings of Metaverse

While such a Metaverse does not yet exist, the components and venues necessary for its creation are coming together.

Axie Infinity, Decentral, and Second Live are all Metaverse-like blockchain-based systems. All of these are online games that let users engage in activities such as playing for money, purchasing and selling virtual property, etc.

In conjunction with other popular digital universe apps such as Fortnite and Roblox, these games have created the closest Metaverse phenomenon to date.

Participants in Roblox, for instance, are not compelled to adhere to a preset storyline. They may also engage in or organize meetings and other social activities. According to reports, people spent around 10 billion hours playing Roblox in the first quarter of 2021, with over 42 million users coming in daily.

For Fortnite, the same can be said. Rather than just playing the game, over 12.3 million users practically attended the Travis Scott performance in Fortnite.

However, experts argue that every organized being's vision of the Metaverse — centralized authority over its digital realities – is diametrically antithetical to what the Metaverse should be.

Jerod Venema, the CEO and Founder of the real-time video communication company Live Switch, says in an article on VentureBeat that all Facebook has to do is to "manage its coders and administrators."

3.3 Centralized vs. Decentralized Metaverse

In comparison to Facebook, Epic Games manages Fortnite, but Roblox Corporation manages Roblox. Given Microsoft's and other centralized businesses' interest in the virtual world, it is clear that the large technology firms now want to lead the push. The Metaverse has become the newest macro-goal for a huge number of the world's top technology behemoths. Epic Games, makers of the Unreal Engine and Fortnite, have said explicitly that this is their purpose. Matthew Ball, the Managing Partner at EpyllionCo and Venture Partner at Makers Fund, wrote in his blog about the Metaverse, "It is also the driving force behind Facebook's acquisition of Oculus VR and its recently launched Horizon virtual world/meeting space, as well as several other initiatives, such as augmented reality glasses and brain-to-machine integrations and interaction."

On the other side, decentralized games such as Axie Infinity, Decentraland, and SecondLife demonstrate how crucial blockchain technology is for smaller businesses to participate fully in the Metaverse.

Due to their open nature, metaverse-like networks are developing into digital economies with various digital currencies and valuables. Additionally, any future iteration of the Metaverse will need to contain these economies, digital identities, and decentralized government, which are all made possible by blockchain technology.

3.4 The Blockchain's Contribution to the Metaverse's Development

Consider a future in which Facebook, Microsoft, Google, and other digital behemoths collaborate on their programs to develop their unique Metaverses.

For instance, a virtual world may arise where users can interact with 3D simulations of WhatsApp, Instagram, and other social services using Facebook's Oculus VR headset.

That 3D virtual universe is unlikely to be connected to Google or Microsoft versions. Even if it is, it is highly implausible that any of these tech titans will let one of them administer and oversee a common Metaverse.

As a result, a decentralized, blockchain-based governance model is taking shape, in which many users, gamers, and community members interact to construct and manage the Metaverse network. The blockchain may store information on user-created virtual locations, the transfer of ownership of digital assets, and financial transactions.

3.5 Crypto in Metaverse

When Facebook rebranded as a meta-network, the Metaverse was the largest concern in IT. Cryptocurrency usage in the Metaverse has been expanding recently, indicating that this is not a fad. We have been on a similar Metaverse path for years, but Facebook's well-publicized move has brought this trend to the fore.

The Metaverse is not only a virtual marketplace for products and NFTs in augmented and mixed reality. This is simply a sliver of the larger picture. This is the next stage of the internet's development, and it will alter every aspect of our life, including our interactions. This part will look at the direction of the trend and, more importantly, how to enter this revolutionary $8 trillion industry as a cryptocurrency and equities markets trader.

It entails the acquisition of Metaverse-specific tokens, which are intrinsically related to the development and commercialization of digital assets. Bear in mind that these Metaverse ecosystems are supported by cryptocurrency and blockchain technology.

Now, we have a slew of stock market participants moving in lockstep. Therefore, let us begin this celebration.

If our descriptions of the Metaverse have left you with any concerns, consider it as a virtual environment in which individuals such as you and me may perform, live, and interact in a variety of settings ranging from performances and seminars to holidays all over the world.

Imagine personalizing a car you are interested in purchasing via the use of VR and holographic technology. Consider using a projector to show your visual art onto the wall of your actual residence. The artwork you possess as one-of-a-kind NFTs is easily verifiable on the blockchain and extremely difficult to duplicate. While your home may burn down or be broken into, your digital assets will stay safe.

Consider attending business meetings from the comfort of your own home, with an encounter that is even better than real life because of the Metaverse's capacity to give an improved, smooth and easy interface. Swiping, touching, or pinching are all possible methods for advancing presentations, opening links, and resizing displays. Consider observing sports from any angle, including that of the athletes. Consider the possibility of being there with your loved ones and exchanging feelings even when you are not physically present.

These are the concerns and preparations of future pioneers, and we are already halfway there. They already have ultrafast broadband, virtual reality goggles, and 24-hour, seven-day-a-week access to online multiplayer worlds.

For many younger people, a transfer to the Metaverse is unnecessary. They are growing up with the expectation that the Metaverse will substantially impact their lives. Whether we like it or not, the remainder of us would have to join.

What role do blockchain technology and cryptocurrencies play in our Metaverse journey? It turns out to be quite a bit. Others believe tomorrow's current crypto entrepreneurs will be the Metaverse's kings. Why is this?

- Because video games are well-established, the Metaverse will very certainly be accessed via them. This will result in a more logical progression.

- The openness of blockchain technology empowers users and fosters creativity.

- Digital tokens, such as cryptocurrency or non-fungible tokens (NFTs), are at the epicenter of the Metaverse change. You are looking at data assets on the blockchain that is controlled by smart contracts.

Chapter 4: Becoming a Part of the Metaverse

After discussing the essential concepts of the Metaverse, let us look at how to join the Metaverse. It will be as simple as putting on their headsets and connecting to the internet for most users. However, you may opt to seek employment in the Metaverse or create a business to increase your portion of the pie before the market gets saturated. Both are attainable goals now, and considering the Metaverse's impact on the future, the time to plan is now.

If you want to work in the Metaverse or establish your own business, you have two choices: participate in the infrastructure construction process or build atop it. One is not always better than the other, and the decision is subjective.

Stability is one of the benefits of working in the metaverse infrastructure. The Metaverse is now being built by tech giants with a crystal clear view of the near future. If you choose to work with them, you will get to work on cutting-edge technology and receive a competitive income and benefits package. Additionally, you will gain invaluable experience and expertise while working, which will come in handy if you decide to start your own business.

However, when it comes to beginning a business, the Metaverse is certainly more profitable. You have a fantastic opportunity to be one of the early entrepreneurs to enter the metaverse industry before it becomes saturated. The infrastructure and market components of the Metaverse will be discussed in terms of career and business options in this chapter. Let us begin by debating how you could contribute to the Metaverse's construction.

4.1 Creating the Metaverse

You may contribute to Metaverse's infrastructure in a variety of ways. Hardware, software, and the content will be used to construct the Metaverse.

Hardware

Even though the hardware is an integral part of the Metaverse, it receives less attention. The Metaverse is devoted to providing the most realistic 3D settings imaginable. Due to the limits of current technology, we require additional hardware to assist us. Virtual reality glasses are commonly associated with Facebook's Oculus, an entrepreneurial success story.

Palmer Luckey, at 15, came up with the concept for Oculus glasses. This is a fantastic example of how a hobby can bloom into a multibillion-dollar enterprise. Luckey acquired an interest in the early prototypes of virtual reality glasses due to his enthusiasm for console gaming. The first virtual reality glasses were created in the 1980s and 1990s. They were either too expensive or just did not work in those days, and as a result, they all failed as company ideas. Luckey began collecting these failed objects as a hobby. He had no clue his curiosity would develop into an in-depth understanding of virtual reality eyewear.

He initiated a crowdfunding campaign to raise funds to create virtual reality spectacles. His initiative sought to generate funding for hardware components and create around one hundred virtual reality spectacles. The target of the campaign was a modest $250,000. However, the Kickstarter campaign raised far more funds. Luckey raised a total of $680,000 in less than 24 hours. That figure topped a million in only three days, catching the attention of industry heavyweights like John Carmack and Gabe Newell. Facebook acquired them for an eye-popping $2 billion in 2014. Zuckerberg's meta looked to have begun to boil at that time.

Luckey's tale teaches us an essential lesson about entrepreneurship in a new field. To begin, time management is key. Neither Luckey nor anybody else invented virtual reality glasses. They were created over decades. Due to Luckey's increased access to technology, he could examine what was not working and develop what would. Second, it is the concept, not the result, that is crucial. Not his Kickstarter prototype, but Luckey's obsession with virtual reality was important in his success.

To summarize, establishing a hardware firm focused on the Metaverse boils down to the first economics lesson taught to every student: supply and demand. The demand must be forecasted and the date of its beginning. Once the market is ready, we give a big population affordable new options. Bear in mind that the basic minimum required for a user to join the Metaverse is hardware. As a result, it will always be vital to the supply chain, with several entry points.

Software

Software is the contemporary world's lifeblood. Without it, the internet world would be unable to give us all of its benefits. Of course, software development will be crucial for both online and offline applications in the Metaverse. You may work in the software industry or start your firm developing software.

The good news for software enthusiasts is that metaverse options are now available. Facebook, Google, Apple, and Snap are all looking for software developers to work on their Metaverse projects. If you are not interested in corporate careers, consider working for one of Metaverse's growing companies, such as Roblox, OpenSea, Decentraland, Niantic, The Sandbox, or Solana. There will always be a significant demand for software developers at all levels in the sector.

When it comes to guiding your career toward the Metaverse, certain programming languages are preferable to others. Distinct programming languages are necessary for augmented reality, virtual reality, blockchain, and cryptocurrency. Your selection will be influenced by the area of the Metaverse in which you are most interested and the language in which you are most at ease.

C# and C++ have a long history for a reason. They are commonly utilized in game development because of their object-oriented nature. Using 3D game engines such as Unity and Unreal, millions worldwide develop surroundings. Another possibility is JavaScript, which gained popularity during Web 2.0 and will continue throughout Web 3.0. If you are interested in developing Web applications, JavaScript is a good choice. Finally, we must not ignore Python, the family's newest member. Python's open-source codebase and scripting features make it an ideal choice for virtual reality applications, which is why companies like Oculus utilize it. Even if you never want to work for another firm, these languages will need to develop your software.

Suppose you are developing software based on metaverse concepts. In that case, it is preferable to collaborate with like-minded individuals since you will need to work swiftly and keep ahead of the competition. Avoid overconfidence in your capacity to compete with large companies, as they will never be completely candid about their research and development. After all, they compete directly with household names. Your efforts might be in vain if they abruptly cease a product you were unaware of. Instead, focus on supply and demand. Which specialized sectors would the main players avoid? Concentrate your efforts on a small number of specific markets.

3D

While all things we discuss are crucial in establishing a metaverse, 3D is the true foundation. This is self-evident: humans experience in three dimensions. That would not be the case if we lived in Carl Sagan's Flatland. Since the human brain interprets the world in three dimensions, virtual reality must be constructed similarly. Even if another reality exists, we would be unable to see it and gain no benefit.

Three-dimensional graphics gained popularity before the Metaverse. On the other side, low-polygon Lara Crofts has passed away. As computer processing capacity rises, 3D technology continues to grow. The ray-tracing technology developed by NVIDIA is an outstanding example of this. It is on the verge of creating environments that are more like real life if they are not already.

Businesses operating in the Metaverse stand to gain the most from the technology's 3D component. However, because of the security and predictability of 3D, there will be fierce competition. If you wait for content mills to take over the market, you will miss out on the benefits of 3D. Establish your studio or freelance business as soon as possible, and use social media to grow your network and recognition.

Niche selection is important to content creator success. When it comes to constructing 3D settings, you have many alternatives. While authentic designs are optimal for architecture, business simulations, and complex game production, cartoon-like designs are optimal for early metaverses and informal game development. Each side offers several advantages and disadvantages; thus, choose the style that best suits your interests and talents. After that, you may choose a niche. Your area of expertise might range from ultra-casual game development to military training. Continue doing what you enjoy since this will assist you in maintaining motivation.

Additionally, if you feel adventurous, you may take on the 3D software component. To create and generate their work, a 3D artist needs software such as Maya. Additionally, 3D modeling programs such as Blender were accessible in the preceding decade, allowing anybody without the artistic ability to create 3D models. Both have become industry standards. There is a good chance that software that directly imports metaverse APIs will be beneficial, as they are the most likely to become industry standards.

Community Management

This is an error of judgment. Although community management may seem insignificant compared to software or hardware development, this is a mistake. Effective community managers will fast become one of Metaverse's most valued assets. We only need to look at the forum culture of Web 2.0 to see this.

When the first forums became available on the web, they immediately gained popularity. Individuals from all across the world may communicate for the first time in history. However, it was the first time they could accomplish this in such a short period. This, without a doubt, paved the way for information freedom. However, some harsh lessons were learned along the road. Regrettably, we discovered these lessons following the commission of real-world crimes while employing internet anonymity.

Moderators and administrators were implemented at that point. They were chosen from among people who spent significant time on the site and expressed an interest in contributing their free time. This was the first time the term "vetting" was used on the internet. The major function of a moderator was to respond promptly to user criticism. Additionally, they can monitor a user's private communications. Different online communities have updated their rules throughout time. While some opted for unrestricted freedom, the majority categorically prohibited hate speech.

When an electronic dispute bleeds into real life, the situation gets more problematic. There has been much debate about whether an online crime may be prosecuted in court. Governments were unprepared for this, resulting in the ambiguous internet prohibitions in place today. Just ask Facebook CEO Mark Zuckerberg, who was recently tasked with explaining the social media industry's workings to the House Financial Services Committee.

This area of the Metaverse can be accessed in a variety of ways. If you are considering a career in law, you may wish to investigate the legal side of the Metaverse. Corporate representation is also an option since major technology businesses pay a premium for attorneys who understand their industry. Alternatively, you might work for non-governmental organizations (NGOs) or lobbyists.

Again, if the law is not your first choice of subject matter, try software. Companies such as Facebook, which administers over a billion accounts, do not choose to employ moderators even though they do so. The true goal is to develop artificial intelligence that can do this role for them. As a result, community management is a promising topic if you are interested in developing artificial intelligence. Additionally, alternative business models are not limited to major firms. By combining artificial intelligence and advisory services for small and medium-sized businesses, you may create an incredible enterprise.

Finance

Finance is another industry that will aid in the growth of the Metaverse. Additionally, anybody is welcome to add to this region of the Metaverse. The only qualifications are the Metaverse, an open mind, and self-taught financial expertise. Acquiring these abilities will enable you to take advantage of extraordinary possibilities.

As mentioned previously, metaverse economies are prone to volatility due to their decentralized nature. This reality generates two commercial prospects. To begin, you may choose to develop a less volatile currency by utilizing a private blockchain. This is not an easy task, but it is fully feasible with the right team and vision. Bear in mind that research and development consume considerable time and money. On the other hand, a strategy that reduces the volatility of the virtual economy would be a game-changer.
The second and more rational path would be to get financial counseling training.

Consider earning a college education to become a financial adviser. However, this is not necessary unless you want to serve in an official role. Making accurate projections is crucial for personal investment and portfolio management in a dynamic market. Additionally, because of the uncertainty around cryptocurrency, some have drawn comparisons to gambling. The economics of the Metaverse remain novel, allowing users to generate tremendous profits. However, as the number of metaverses grows, they will require services to keep their economies afloat. Additionally, governments will want to regulate them to guarantee that tax rules are followed.

As a result, you are not bound by conventional financial rules. Alternatively, you may pursue a strategy that is centered on software. With a thorough understanding of blockchain technology, you can offer a varied range of services to meet the changing demands of the new economy. Along with creating unique blockchains, you can also develop ground-breaking smart contracts. Following that, you may alter user agreement and privacy policy templates, both of which are key components of Web 3.0.

Finally, you may develop your economy. While creating and maintaining a cryptocurrency involves teamwork, creating altcoins is straightforward. However, this industry necessitates a significant degree of exposure. By the beginning of 2022, there are expected to be more than 5,000 altcoins. Crypto aficionados refer to these currencies as "shitcoins" owing to their inability to work properly and lack of value. That does not have to be the case. Are you familiar with Dogecoin? Elon Musk's involvement in it resulted in a wave of millionaires. While hiring Elon Musk to assist with public relations is not always feasible, we can learn from this experience. It can work rather effectively if your cryptocurrency serves a function and is well-known within the relevant groups.

4.2 Joining the Metaverse

While constructing a metaverse may not be your cup of tea, you might build on previously created work. The following concepts will revolutionize certain sectors and create new employment and business possibilities.

Organizing an occasion

Virtual reality has the potential to transform the way events are organized significantly. As one of the pioneering studios, you may provide virtual events. Concerts or talks may be held as part of the festivities. You must organize, promote, and maintain the software to assure the success of your virtual event planning business.

You can work with event organizers or make alliances with other creatives to start your own business. It is conditional on the nature of the occurrence. In general, a virtual reality constructor is suitable for private meetings, seminars, and concerts. However, if you want to take your events to the next level, you need to develop some coding skills.

Consider the iconic Holodeck from Star Trek. The Holodeck is the spacecraft Enterprise's most popular feature. That is unsurprising. It is an empty 3D environment in which you may run any software. You may assume the persona of Sherlock Holmes, travel back in time to discuss mathematics with Einstein and travel to several universes. Essentially, you are free to run wild with your imagination. If you want this kind of specialized event planning, you will require some serious software. This is precisely why technology giants like Google are recruiting engineers to work on their augmented reality initiatives. Augmented reality will be the future of event planning in Web 3.0.

Consulting

A consultant role is suitable if you have a firm handle on the Metaverse. The consulting industry has shifted dramatically in the digital age. As previously said, the big participants had no clue how significant Web 1.0 would become when it started. Simply ask Yahoo, which was compelled to pay $5.7 billion to acquire Marc Cuban's media company. They certainly would have performed better with the guidance of a competent consultant.

Prepare now if you are considering a career as a metaverse consultant. Maintain an awareness of current events and learn how to analyze data if you have not previously. Connect with as many people as possible and work your cold pitches. I adopt the role of a metaverse consultant through blogging, social networking, and as a guest author.

Many business owners are currently fearful of Web 3.0. They do not want to repeat Web 2.0's errors, and you can substantially influence enterprises. There is no reason to wait for virtual worlds and blockchain technology to become more widely used. Smart contracts, cryptocurrencies, network effect transistors, and virtual land are all available for integration into any business.

Create a non-profit organization to aid artists in securing their digital copyrights. You provide low-cost programming services for smart contracts. Make first contact with venture capital companies and serve as a link between them and Metaverse startups. Conduct cryptocurrency investment seminars. The trick is to fall in love with, comprehend, and believe in some facet of the Metaverse. Later on, the business concept will emerge.

Virtual Property

Since the birth of civilization, real estate has been lucrative employment and investment opportunity. The justification for investing in real estate is self-evident. The earth is not becoming extinct. A valuable piece of land will always create value and provide prospects for growth. The virtual worlds of the Metaverse follow a similar structure. The boundlessness of these landscapes adds to their allure. Virtual lands will be available for purchase, sale, and development as long as users create virtual worlds.

There are several specializations available in virtual land and real estate. One of the most apparent possibilities is to become a virtual land agent. You may invest in the virtual world by acting as a broker between landowners and investors. Users are likely to feel both compelled and anxious at the start of the Metaverse. After all, virtual land is opposed to what people are accustomed to. If you have great communication skills and a working grasp of money, you may become a valuable asset. The value of virtual real estate is pretty high.

Alternatively, you may pursue a career as a contractor. A metaverse engineer would be endowed with extraordinary abilities. The Golden Gate Bridge is a marvel of contemporary architecture, but only in a virtual reality in which the laws of physics can be altered to resemble anything. The possibilities are truly endless. Take Minecraft into consideration! The business model is in place. Users may now create customized environments using SimLab's virtual reality creation software, Composer. NASA, Tesla, Nike, Sony, and Volvo are just a few of their illustrious clients.

Finally, let us not forget about land flipping. Successful land flipping entails first becoming used to the virtual world. After determining the property's location and the locations where people are likely to congregate, you may invest in virtual land. This may involve some investment, but it will pay off handsomely if you successfully improve the value of your land. Creating a business on your property may boost its value and turn it into an attractive advertising location. The trick is to be creative. When the land achieves its maximum worth, you may sell it and invest in further land to resume the process. Additionally, you may rent the property or contract the work out to a contractor.

A virtual business

We can evaluate Metaverse's small business potential based on the provided data. During its peak, Second Life featured a bustling economy of tiny companies. Individuals have capitalized on this by developing side hustles, some of which have grown into full-time jobs.

In most virtual worlds, users join the area using an avatar. Our avatars can perform all of the jobs that we are capable of performing in reality and more. They travel, work, mingle, and create romantic relationships in addition to eating, sleeping, and seeking entertainment. Fortunately, you will be there to meet their needs.

Your metaverse business does not need to be complicated. Even something as simple as running a coffee shop on a busy street may be highly lucrative. One of the key benefits of managing a business in the Metaverse is creating in-game currency. Cryptocurrency funds can be stored indefinitely or exchanged for fiat currencies. You may earn additional revenue by presenting stand-up comedy and jam sessions with live music. Additionally, coffee shops serve as good meeting places. You may offer a job board for other businesses and users or rent out advertising space in your coffee shop.

You may always go to Second World and customize high-end things if you choose. There is no reason why you cannot be Gucci's of the Metaverse. The enthralling component of virtual worlds is individuals' emotional bonds with their avatars. They regard them as a more truthful portrayal of themselves. Popmundo, a well-known virtual roleplaying community in which participants could assume the persona of a rock star, was an excellent example of this. Even if you are not generating music, you may still influence your band's creative and financial issues. Individuals were prepared to pay for VIP services only to enhance their avatars. Spending irresponsibly on/as your avatar is an infrequent occurrence that you should avoid. Purchasing items for your avatar on an irregular basis is rather common for average users. The bulk of users will demand products that any other user does not own. Profit from this perspective and earn a respectable chunk of money.

A coffee shop and a boutique offering personalized products are just two examples of small companies that may thrive in a virtual world. Your only limitation is your imagination. Even if you are not interested in establishing a whole corporation, you may be compelled by metaverse enterprises. The good news is that you do not have to create your own business; you can just invest in one. To that end, we will explore Metaverse's business operations.

Chapter 5: Investing in Metaverse

The Metaverse is here, representing the next stage in the internet's growth. As a result, we will probably be unable to access digital information via smartphones or computers shortly, as these gadgets will become outdated. However, we will entirely be immersed in a virtual environment and will be able to communicate with individuals from all over the world using smart glasses. Whether you like it or not, the industry is coming, it is going to happen, and it will be worth $850 billion by 2030. When it comes to enterprises, what are the stocks of firms in which we may invest to benefit from the Metaverse's growth?

The Metaverse can be described in many ways, yet each definition boils down to the same concept or idea. It has become the current global hot subject. The Metaverse is a collaborative virtual reality environment that can be accessed via smart glasses and is completely immersive. Our connections will be multifaceted in this climate. How do we now engage with one another? We communicate on social media in two-dimensional or, at most, three-dimensional worlds, similar to those found in certain online games. However, due to the Metaverse, human interactions will be multi-dimensional in four dimensions, allowing individuals to immerse themselves in digital material rather than simply seeing it.

When wearing virtual reality glasses and entering a virtual environment, it is feasible to dance with someone halfway around the world. To a greater extent, similar to the Matrix, you might go surfing in the desert or somewhere else. The Metaverse will drastically transform how we work, play, and learn in the future. For instance, how do you envision yourself working in the future? The applications will no longer be available through laptop or tablet; instead, you will put on the glasses, and the programs will appear across your environment.

Do you recall Tom Cruise's Minority Report program, in which he was constantly swiping and expanding objects, or even how Tony Stark handled it in Iron Man when you had to move things about with the hologram? What occurs in the Metaverse is precise, as I expected. Our applications will be distributed across the environment, and we will be able to drag and drop files into and out of our virtual area. Consider the idea of future encounters in which we will be able to interact with individuals from all over the world via avatars at any location we choose.

Consider that these advancements may imply that zoom, smartphones, and tablets may become obsolete shortly, and you will not be astonished. Consider the likelihood that firms such as Apple or Samsung will not make a future pivot to this Metaverse. Due to the quick speed of technological advancement, their products may become as outdated as video cassettes were in the past.

More exciting is how the Metaverse may transform our interactions with video games. According to the Facebook video, which was termed "meta," you could fence with someone from another country by donning a set of virtual reality glasses. You see their avatar, they notice you, and the two of you begin fencing.

Education, too, can be fascinating. Consider donning those smart glasses and seeing into a human body, touching a human heart, and witnessing how organs communicate. Atoms may be swiped, and the cosmos expands in outer space due to your deeds. It is going to be amazing.

Another industry has been found with a projected value of nearly one trillion dollars by 2028. Interestingly, some of the world's most well-known firms are already taking this seriously and developing their presence in the Metaverse. For example, Nike is quietly designing new products in preparation for the Metaverse. They have submitted seven trademark applications to offer branded virtual footwear and clothes in the Metaverse.

Again, in the future, in Metaverse, we will have an avatar and will be able to communicate with individuals from all over the world. To enhance your avatar's appearance, you may purchase Nike footwear, apparel, and sweaters. According to Nike, you will be able to purchase them in the virtual world. They are now manufacturing all of these virtual Nike products, not just for Nike but for Gucci and other luxury brands.

Gucci has also offered digital accessories, apparel, and handbags on the Roblox game platform. What is Roblox exactly? Roblox is a virtual environment that resembles the Metaverse quite a bit. It is a gaming environment that is accessible over the internet. Individuals are already engaged in this online gaming world, acquiring Gucci clothes, trading them, and transacting virtual retail activities. They recently launched a Gucci garden on Roblox, which you can view here. Some individuals were likely able to resale Gucci products on the internet for as low as one dollar to nine dollars, including Gucci glasses, Gucci bags, and Gucci clothes. They acquired it for $4.75 and then sold the Gucci bag, a virtual digital bag, for $4,000 on the Roblox website. Millions will be created in the Metaverse, just as millions will be made in the actual world. Today, brands and organizations are taking this seriously because they recognize that it is no longer a fad or a fabrication of their imagination. This is a real occurrence. Brands will need to enter the Metaverse to be relevant in the future.

Investing in the Metaverse may likely prove to be one of the most spectacular opportunities in the future for astute investors to make a large sum of money. Following Facebook's recent rebranding to meta to further develop its vision and interpretation of the Metaverse, the company has piqued investors' interest in how they can potentially invest early and profit from what could be an incredible investment opportunity.

Indeed, several intriguing and diversified ways to invest in the Metaverse go beyond standard stock market investing. As the Metaverse becomes increasingly incorporated into our daily lives, it piques our attention. It exists in a more virtual world, and I am sure that the investment opportunities linked with it will continue to expand in scope over time. This section will discuss various early investment options.

5.1 Stocks

The very first investment opportunity I would like to discuss is stock investing. It is the principal source of income for most investment portfolios, including mine. Additionally, various firms are actively contributing to the Metaverse and the infrastructure required for the metaverse ecosystem's development.

Our knowledge base already has information on Mark Zuckerberg's intentions to develop his Metaverse and stake a claim on the future growth of social networking. In this scenario, however, it is important emphasizing that the Metaverse itself is far larger than the capabilities of a single firm, both in terms of the infrastructure necessary to build it and the activities that will take place inside it.

It comprises various activities, including gaming with friends in a virtual environment, attending live events and entertainment, receiving personal training without visiting a gym, collaborating with coworkers and conducting meetings in a virtual workplace, and even shopping in the Metaverse. Consider the numerous businesses operating, developing, and possessing a physical product that they may convert to a digital or virtual product and place in the Metaverse.

Gaming firms include Unity software and Roblox. Peloton is a workout firm. Zoom and Microsoft are examples of video conferencing companies. Amazon and Shopify are examples of e-commerce companies. All of the firms listed previously provide several probabilities. As a result, there are multiple ways to invest in and obtain exposure to some of these stocks as part of a diversified investment portfolio plan. It will be intriguing to observe which stocks opt to invest in the firm to acquire exposure to the Metaverse and aggressively make market share.

The market potential, or anticipated market opportunity, for the Metaverse is estimated to reach 825 billion dollars by 2028, growing at a compounded annual growth rate of 43.3 percent each year. The Metaverse has abundant investment opportunities for businesses that can benefit from tremendous development by investing in it and delivering some form of virtual product within it.

How much of a company's stock will be necessary to create, build, and maintain the Metaverse and benefit from the internet's next evolution? Hundreds of stocks will benefit from the Metaverse, but I will focus on the most critical ones and group them as crucial metaverse stocks.

Corporate Entities

Businesses involved in developing hardware, operating systems, and metaverse software would fall under the first category. These are firms that are building smart glasses and advancing them and the operating system that will power the Metaverse's virtual reality environment. Additionally, we will include firms responsible for the construction and maintenance of Metaverse's infrastructure, which will be achieved via cloud computing. There are various firms; however, I am going to focus on the following:

Meta

If you have not lived under a rock, you are undoubtedly already aware that Facebook has changed its name to Meta. What rationale behind Facebook's meta-branding? According to its mission statement, its long-term strategic objective is to be the dominating player in the Metaverse. Due to their ownership of the Oculus VR headsets, games, and virtual reality headgear, they have a huge technological edge over their competitors in terms of hardware and software.

Their cooperation with Ray-ban led to the development of Ray-ban Tales, the company's most recent smart eyewear edition. They are the leaders of the pack. Microsoft has moved into a close second place, and the two companies are collaborating on Meta.

Microsoft

Additionally, Microsoft's CEO announced that the corporation would develop Metaverse's enterprise component. That is where they anticipate professionals gathering, collaborating, and cooperating in the future, much as they do now inside a virtual environment filled with avatars. Additionally, Microsoft has invested in its smart glasses, the Hololens.

Amazon

Amazon has also disclosed its intentions to enter the Metaverse, where it intends to develop a virtual economy and virtual stores that consumers may visit while in the virtual economy. For instance, if you consider purchasing a shirt, you may utilize Virtual Tryons to ensure that it fits properly. Cloud computing services are essential for Metaverse's infrastructure construction and maintenance. Amazon Web Services and Microsoft Azure are the market's two most dominant companies. Additionally, there are online alphabet services accessible. All of these are required to construct and maintain the Metaverse's infrastructure.

The instruments employed in the content development process

A single organization or individual cannot develop the Metaverse. It will be built collaboratively by millions of computer programmers, designers, and developers worldwide. It will be a global collaborative effort like Wikipedia. As a result, these individuals will require tools to develop Metaverse content, such as virtual real estate, virtual buildings, and virtual avatars. What are the names of the companies that provide the technologies necessary to create these metaverse environments? The first is the ticker symbol ADSK, abbreviating Autodesk.

Autodesk

Autodesk is the world's largest software producer for architects, engineers, and construction industry professionals.

Before a builder begins construction on a physical project, they create designs using 3D modeling software called AutoCAD. Autodesk has announced a collection of tools that enable computer programmers to create virtual reality and augmented reality 3D structures and simulations, such as virtual reality and augmented reality buildings and infrastructure.

Autodesk is, of course, a necessary piece of software for anybody interested in developing metaverse environments. The next stock to investigate would be the Roblox company's ticker symbol RBLX.

Roblox

Roblox is an online gaming platform with 164 million monthly active users. You could utilize Roblox to develop your own game if you want to. Additionally, you may create your games and contribute to those created by others. These games are comparable to those in which you interact with other players via an avatar. You may use them to sell stuff and purchase commodities from other users, and the site features a native Roblox money that acts similarly to a virtual economy.

As with the Gucci bag that can be purchased digitally within the Roblox virtual environment, the Roblox platform will be a necessary tool for people wishing to create games in the Metaverse, just as the Gucci bag in the real world. The following stock will be discussed: Unity software, indicated by the letter U.

Software developed by Unity

Additionally, Unity will be a vital tool for programmers developing metaverse games in the future. As the leading designers of 3D video game engines, they are in charge of customizing how video game players move and interact with their games. 94 out of every 100 game development firms utilize the Unity engine. Unity would be critical in supporting firms in developing distinctive metaverse presences and environments. They have access to professional software and gaming service tools. Along with these firms, there are others, such as Tech Two Interactive, Electronic Arts, and Metapod. There are a few more stocks to examine, but these are the most critical.

Semiconductors

Since semiconductors are the essential building blocks of any digital economy, avoiding them is difficult. To keep the Metaverse functioning, many semiconductors will be required. Today, a slew of semiconductor stocks is offered. The first category would consist of semiconductor companies specializing in the design of high-end chips.

Nvidia

Nvidia is the market leader, while AMD is also a viable option. There are a few more in addition to Nvidia, but Nvidia is the most well-known high-end CPU architecture. The chips are designed entirely by Nvidia. They do not manufacture the chips. So who manufactures these high-end chips? Taiwan Semiconductor Manufacturing Company, symbol TSMC, is responsible for 90% of these high-end, complex chips with a diameter of fewer than five nanometers.

Although other semiconductor companies have strong ties to Nvidia and TSMC, such as ASML, Applied Materials, Alarm Research, and many more, Nvidia and TSMC would be the two leading contenders.

These are the critical stocks to hold if you want to benefit from the Metaverse's imminent advent. If you are interested in investing in an Exchange-traded Fund (ETF), there is also a metaverse ETF available. The Metaverse ETF is the costliest and has the thickest symbol, which is Meta.

5.2 How to Invest in Stocks Successfully?

Successful investing entails more than simply knowing what to buy. You may already know what you want to buy, but this is insufficient. When developing into a successful investor, there are four factors to keep in mind. They include the following:

You must be knowledgeable about the product you are purchasing.

You must understand the optimal timing to purchase the stock. You must be informed of the appropriate quantity of shares to purchase.

You must be able to choose when to sell and when to collect your profits.

Many people face the dilemma of knowing exactly what they want to buy but purchasing it at the wrong time. They purchase a stock when it is seen to be overvalued, overpriced, or overextended, among other criteria. As a result, merely knowing what to buy is insufficient; you must also know when to purchase it. For instance, when it comes to investing, you only need to purchase these businesses' stock when it is much cheaper.

For instance, whereas Meta, or Facebook, is today undervalued and Nvidia is overvalued, TSMC, with the ticker symbol TSM, a Taiwan Semiconductor Manufacturing business, is currently undervalued. Thus, you must understand which stocks are undervalued and overvalued, as investing in an overpriced stock might result in a loss of money.

How would you identify a company's true worth and calculate its intrinsic value? It is an excellent time to buy when a stock is inexpensive and prices have retraced to a chart support level. You must study the technical charts when timing your entrance. It all boils down to how well your entries are timed. The company is excellent, but it is pricey, and the stock is currently overvalued. Before making a trade, the market should retrace closer to a support level.

Additionally, keep in mind that there are certain equities in which you are not required to invest but may trade for a short amount of time. I like to invest in profitable companies and generate cash flow to determine their real value. However, some stocks are not profitable and continue to lose money, so I would avoid investing in them, but they do have the potential to appreciate.

These are stocks that are meant to be traded on a short-term basis. If you are going to trade, you should understand how to place your stop loss and profit target and how to join and exit trades with the maximum profit and the least risk. Additionally, how can you utilize options to mitigate risk while enhancing reward? As an example, use caution because both Roblox and Unity are unprofitable at the publication time. They continue to incur losses, and their stock is vastly inflated. While you should avoid investing in these stocks directly, you should consider using options to execute a short-term swing trade on them.

5.3 Tokens for Use in Metaverse

Following that, a few further investment opportunities are slightly more appealing. As a result, we are going to begin by discussing metaverse tokens. For instance, a website such as coinmarketcap.com enables you to travel to and click on the metaverse page, which lists some of the most popular metaverse cryptocurrency currencies.

We have a variety of tokens, including Axie Infinity, Decentraland, Enjin money, and the Sandbox. These have varying market capitalizations, most notably axie infinite and Decentraland, which have market capitalizations ranging from nearly $6 billion to over $9 billion. These are hardly inconsequential trinkets. They are digital tokens in which many individuals are investing actively. These tokens are essentially the same as the currency used in the corresponding virtual metaverses they have developed for you to explore.

I suppose you might compare spending a lot of money in England to buy items. The same may be stated for these so-called virtual or metaverse worlds. For instance, the AXS token is linked to Axie Infinity, the MANA token to Decentraland, and the SAN token to Sandbox.

These tokens are garnering investors' interest. Because they believe their Metaverse will be the next big thing, they are using the tokens to purchase items within it and are looking to invest in this token as a pure investment opportunity. It is incredible to observe how much the value of these metaverse tokens has soared in the months after Facebook announced its rebranding. The Decentraland token's price climbed by 75% in a year, hitting a market high of $3.56. As of today's market price, the token is selling at around $3.17 per token, which is a comparatively low price compared to major cryptocurrencies such as bitcoin.

By investing in these metaverse tokens, you are betting on the linked Metaverse's popularity increasing over time. As demand increases, you will be able to purchase more items within the Metaverse, resulting in a gradual price increase.
When it comes to investing in some of these metaverse tokens, subjectivity plays a role. Decentraland now has a market value of $6 billion, but what constitutes a billion dollars?

It is all about supply and demand and potential competitors inside the market. However, due to the complexity of certain of these tokens, it remains hard to assign an underlying value to them. I feel that the upside potential for some of these crypto-built metaverses, particularly given their predicted ascent, may be astronomical.

5.4 Land & Property

My usage of "land and property" does not imply a standard definition of land and property. I refer to land and property in some of the newly constructed metaverses. You could purchase pixels that represented land and ownership rights within these metaverses.

We are all aware of Disney's magnificent investment a few decades ago when he acquired 27000 acres of property in Orlando, Florida, a bargain at the time for around $182 per acre. Today, the land is worth several billion dollars, and a similar scenario appears in the Metaverse. You would be surprised how much money some of this land is currently selling for if you understood its true value. We may purchase land in the sandbox metaverse by clicking on the buy land button. This then redirects us to a platform where many individuals may purchase NFTs and other forms of digital assets. By glancing at them, you can realize how expensive some of these regions are. It is an absurd circumstance.

According to the recently sold part, lawful land is selling for between 1.5 and 2 Ethereum, depending on the property's theme. That is most likely valued somewhere in the market at

$4500. The price of land can go to around $9,000 for a few pixels on a computer screen. After you have acquired the property, it will appear on the metaverse map, along with various other symbols signifying individuals who have purchased land inside the firm.

Another video game company appears to have acquired sandbox metaverse property, this time to make games. Individuals and potential enterprises may be discovered in their hundreds around the Metaverse who have acquired land in the sandbox metaverse.

You may be wondering how investing in this land and purchasing land within these metaverses constitutes a financial opportunity, and I understand your misunderstanding. As previously indicated, as the number of people who use this Metaverse and its tokens increases, the quantity of land accessible for purchase becomes increasingly restricted due to the high demand. At this moment, the concept of supply and demand is effectively established. Due to a limited supply, individuals can demand any price they feel they can sell their property for.

What is exciting is that you may continue to build on your already-established landing. If you decide to sell the land later, you may be able to command a greater price for it since it would be more interesting to potential buyers if it had more infrastructure. Suppose you consider yourself a somewhat astute landowner and investor in some of these metaverses. In that case, you should investigate some of the marketplaces accessible on these various metaverses to see what you can discover.

5.5 Wearables and Non Fungible Tokens (NFTs)

Non-fungible tokens are objects that, while some believe have no worth in the physical world, have the potential to have enormous value when utilized and applied in the virtual world. This is especially true if you are migrating as a human species from valuing physical goods and items to valuing digital assets and items, such as cryptocurrencies. You may be the only owner of an NFT, which you may install in your virtual property to sit on the virtual land in your Metaverse, where people are now flexing in their fine attire and expensive vehicles. With NFTs and wearables, you may observe similar events in the Metaverse as you do in the real world. It is a fascinating concept that is almost certainly mind-boggling to consider for a time.

5.6 Opportunities for Market Development in the Metaverse

Generally, I imagine that these metaverses will be utilized by many 12-year-olds who will run around in their virtual worlds with their avatars, but the reality is very different. The amount of money spent on these platforms is genuinely staggering, and contemplating its magnitude is mind-boggling.

Consider the following illustration: On-axis affinity, the most expensive item ever sold was 300 Ethereum, worth around

1.35 million dollars or over a million pounds sterling at today's market price. The sums being spent on some of these digital assets are absurd. It has been observed in the NFT realm, and it is now beginning to be observed in these metaverses as well, which is interesting. This is a huge investment opportunity if you know what you are doing and which assets to invest in, as some of them are certainly quite valuable. On a similar note, you may also encounter what are referred to as wearables in these virtual worlds.

Consider the following scenario: you are a virtual environment user with an avatar. To complete the appearance, you will need to accessorize the avatar with numerous accessories and one-of-a-kind items only accessible to that avatar. Consider one of the Metaverse's markets to illustrate what I mean.

You may discover a broad selection of NFT, wearables, and collectibles in the Decentraland marketplace that you can actively employ to personalize your avatar's look.

You can see the various price tokens for the various variables, ranging from 70 to 1500 tokens and, in some cases, as few as five tokens. Their rarity mostly determines the value of these diverse digital assets. Thus, you have graduated from common assets that you may purchase to unique ones that are one-of-a-kind collections, like the one below, a 2500 token Ethereum dusk ghost helmet valued at around $7,500 in actual cash.

It is one of those things subject to supply and demand, even more so if the item you are purchasing is a little unusual. When more people start using the Metaverse, the price of those uncommon items will increase in value as demand grows and more people start using these metaverses. Due to the scarcity of uncommon items, their worth will increase as demand grows and more individuals begin to use these metaverses. These are just a handful of the numerous ways you might invest in the future of one or more of these metaverses.

Chapter 6: NFT Investing in the Metaverse

NFT technology, which is still a relatively new phenomenon on the blockchain in 2022, ensures ownership of virtual assets and has been used most prominently (or infamously) in digital art, to mention a few examples. In comparison to past years, there was a notable focus on the future of NFTs in 2022, which many believe will be in their use as critical components in the next version of the internet, dubbed Web 3.0 or "Web3." Eventually, it is envisaged that by merging this platform with NFTs, a huge, decentralized virtual world known as the "metaverse" would be created.

Money units are fungible and interchangeable in the cryptocurrency world, just as they are in the real world, but not all digital assets are. In this case, NFTs are advantageous. The digitization of content — including art, music, film, literature, and even news or blog pieces — has rendered obsolete traditional notions of ownership, copyright, and intellectual property protection. This is mostly due to the ease with which digital material may be duplicated and recreated. On the other hand, NFTs enable owners of various digital properties to sell and trade their assets while using the decentralized crypto environment's benefits. This summer, a twelve-year-old in the United Kingdom made almost $400,000.

He did it by coding some virtual NFT art. It was sold for more than $1 million in an auction for an NFT resembling ownership of a single square pixel. If such charges sound too expensive, consider that an American graphic designer spent $69 million for a significantly more complex digital NFT artwork. While extravagant expenditure is not uncommon in the art world, thousands of dollars for a computer file that anybody can easily reproduce is unique. Was there a misunderstanding here? The application of NFT technology to the ownership of digital art may be viewed as a warm-up for the future diffusion of NFTs to other types of assets. For example, McDonald's and Burger King are experimenting with digital "collectibles," which are virtual representations of tangible objects.

On the other hand, the gaming sector may serve as the primary incubator for NFTs. The online gaming sector is already substantial in income, having eclipsed the popularity of films, music, and sports. Numerous games, including those that use NFTs, have already incorporated blockchain technology into their gameplay. The gameplay in games such as Axie Infinity enables users to create virtual NFT animals with unique characteristics that can be traded for real bitcoin. In Upland's asset trading game, users participate in a digital real estate market in which NFTs represent geolocated plots using real-world GPS coordinates.

These games exemplify how NFTs may be used to symbolize assets in a somewhat large-scale, more flexible virtual environment, such as the Metaverse.

While NFTs have a bright future, they are not difficult to implement. While the Ethereum blockchain now serves as the foundation for most NFTs, this gap is decreasing as competitors like the significantly faster Solana blockchain gain prominence. Ethereum has several challenges, including scalability, cost, and performance. These vulnerabilities will be resolved as part of the Ethereum 2.0 upgrade, scheduled to occur in 2022. This, however, is subject to change in light of recent delays. Numerous technologies that would comprise the Metaverse's basis, including the Web3 network, NFTs, and cryptocurrencies, would need to develop and expand in phases, much like the internet's backbone did during its early 1990s.

6.1 What are NFTs

A non-fungible token, or NFT, is a form of the data unit that is non-transferable and unique and is kept on a blockchain, a digital ledger used to record transactions. NFTs can be used to connect digital commodities such as photos, movies, and audio that can be duplicated. NFTs establish ownership by using a digital ledger kept by the NFT.

However, they do not restrict the exchange or duplication of the computer's real digital data. Non-fungible tokens (NFTs) are distinct from other blockchain-based cryptocurrencies such as Bitcoin in the sense that they are not interchangeable (fungible).

Non-fungible tokens (NFTs) have come under fire for the significant carbon footprint and energy expenses associated with confirming blockchain transactions and their widespread usage in art fraud.

Additionally, there are concerns regarding the utility of creating evidence of ownership in an unregulated market that is often outside the legal system's authority. When you exchange one bitcoin for another, you will receive the identical thing; this is referred to as a bitcoin's fungibility. On the other hand, a restricted trade card is not transportable and exchanging it for another card results in an entirely different card. Non-fungible tokens (also known as NFTs) are digital assets on a blockchain. They are thus different from other digital assets under their unique identification codes and information. Unlike other cryptocurrencies, they cannot be exchanged or switched at face value. It displays a lack of concern about cryptocurrencies, which are all identical and may be used in the future to facilitate financial transactions.

Bitcoin and other cryptocurrencies are fungible and can be traded or exchanged just like actual money. For example, the value of a single Bitcoin will always be equal to the value of another Bitcoin. As a result, one Either is perpetually identical to one Ether unit and vice versa. Cryptocurrencies are well-suited for use as a secure payment mechanism in the virtual economy, where their fungibility has helped them gain widespread popularity.

Each NFT is irreplaceable and unique, disrupting the cryptographic norm and making it nearly difficult to treat an NFT and a fungible token interchangeably. Since each token has a unique, non-transferable identity that distinguishes it from all other tokens in circulation, tokens have been compared to digital passports. They are also extendible, implying that by breeding two NFTs together, a third NFT wholly distinct from the original two may be developed. Like Bitcoin, NFTs have ownership information that enables token holders to be easily recognized and tokens to be traded between owners without using a third party. NFTs enable asset owners to provide pertinent information or attributes about the item being traded. For coffee beans, for example, fair trade tokens displaying the beans may be recognized as proof of provenance.

NFTs were developed as a result of the ERC-721 standard. ERC-721 was built by the same individuals that produced ERC-20. It defines the minimal interface required for the exchange and assignment of gaming tokens, including information about their ownership, security, and metadata. The ERC-1155 standard lowers the storage and transaction costs associated with NFTs by encapsulating them in a single contract.

Probably the most well-known application of NFTs is by crypto cats. Cryptokitties, first presented in November 2017, were blockchain-based digital representations of kittens with individual identities. Each kitten is priced individually and is one-of-a-kind. These creatures mate amongst themselves and generate offspring with individual characteristics and values from their parents. Crypto kittens quickly gained popularity, with fans spending more than $20 million in Ethereum to purchase, feed, and care for kittens during their first few days.

According to reports, some devotees invested more than $100,000 in the endeavor. While the initial usage of crypto-kitties may appear trivial, the subsequent ones have far-reaching commercial ramifications. NFTs have been employed in stock investments and real estate transactions. Incorporating several token types into a single contract has several ramifications: the possibility to function as an escrow for various non-fungible tokens, ranging from artwork to real estate, all inside the same financial transaction. Each NFT has a unique structure, which enables it to be used in various applications. Especially well-suited is digital representations of actual assets such as artwork and real estate. They may also eliminate intermediaries, link artists and audiences, and even manage user identities, as they are built on blockchains. NFTs have the potential to eliminate intermediaries, simplify transactions, and create new markets.

Sports cards, digital artworks, and rare things all contribute significantly to the present market for NFTs. NBA Top Shot, where you can purchase NBA NFTs via digital cards, is the most talked-about location. Many of these cards fetched millions of dollars at auction. "I am just getting started with Twitter," Jack Dorsey said in the first tweet posted on the social media platform. The NFT of the first tweet in history drew offers of up to 2.5 million dollars.

An NFT is nothing more than a data unit stored on a blockchain that can be purchased and traded on the cryptocurrency market. When an NFT is associated with a real or virtual asset, the asset may be used for a specified purpose, and the NFT may be used to grant authorization for the asset's ownership for that purpose. On the digital marketplace, an NFT may be purchased and traded. Typically, the nonlegal disposition of NFT operations results in an informal transfer of property over an object that lacks a legal foundation for implementation and typically confers little more than the ability to operate as a social status item. NFTs are similar to cryptographic tokens in that they fulfill the same goal.

6.2 Importance of NFTs

non-fungible tokens represent a significant advancement over the relatively straightforward notion of bitcoin. Modern finance systems incorporate complex trade and finance infrastructures for various asset classes, including real estate investment, loan contracts, and artwork. NFTs, by enabling the creation of virtual replicas of real assets, represents a significant step toward reestablishing this infrastructure. The digital representation of tangible assets or unique identifiers is not novel.

When it comes to a wine bottle, it will be simpler for the many actors in the current chain to collaborate using an NFT. It will aid in the traceability of the bottle's origin, manufacture, and sale. This approach, developed by the consulting company Ernst & Young, has already proven advantageous to one of the firm's clients. As previously noted, NFTSs are also suited for use in identity management. Consider the example of authentic passports, which must be shown at entry and exit points.

Additionally, NFTs may be utilized for identity and access control in the digital realm, extending on the prior purpose. Along with real estate, this tokenization approach may be used for other assets, such as artwork, without being limited to real estate. As a result, artwork does not have to be possessed by a single individual to be legitimate. Numerous individuals have access to the digital version of the artwork, each of whom is accountable for a distinct painting region. These types of partnerships may help a business increase its value and income. For non-financial companies, the most intriguing prospect for the foreseeable future is the creation of new marketplaces and forms of investment.

Consider a vast piece of land that has been divided into multiple sections, each with its own set of characteristics and various sorts of property. In one of the portions, there may be a beach, an entertainment complex, or a residential neighborhood nearby. Each NFT represents a distinct piece of real estate. Each parcel of land is valued differently based on its traits apart from the others. Including crucial information in each NFT makes it possible to simplify real estate dealing, a hard and bureaucratic endeavor. For instance, Decentraland, a blockchain-based virtual reality platform that runs on the Ethereum network, has already implemented this notion. Non-financial tokens (NFTs) are maturing and becoming more incorporated into the financial system. Tokenized hunks of land with varied values and locations may be applied to genuine plots of land for real estate.

6.3 Why NFTs Are Required for Metaverse Access?

Individuals and businesses have nearly endless options for transferring physical products and services to virtual equivalents in digital three-dimensional environments.
Specifically, the gaming economy is based on the concept of play-to-earn. It will engage and empower gamers of

blockchain games via non-fungible tokens (NFTs), which the blockchain will enable.

Specifically, the gaming economy is based on the concept of play-to-earn. It will engage and empower gamers of blockchain games via non-fungible tokens (NFTs), which the blockchain will enable.

NFTs provide a portal to the Metaverse, allowing for constructing identities, communities, and social experiences.

With the increasing number of uses for NFTs, these digital assets herald the beginning of a new era in the virtual world known as the Metaverse. The advent of metaverses on the global stage is best demonstrated by Facebook's launch of Meta, which heralds the beginning of a new era in which Augmented experiences powered by NFTs will provide the basis for next-generation social media platforms.

NFTs and metaverses are already inextricably linked, most notably in blockchain gaming and some other interoperable games, where they serve as value carriers in the expansion of digital social media. This is particularly true in the case of other interoperable games and blockchain-based gaming. While this is a relatively new concept, this new gaming arm has surpassed $16 million in trade volume in less than two weeks, with every NFT collection sold out.

6.4 Role of NFTs and blockchain in Metaverse

Many people believe that NFTs are just photographs of artworks or treasures, which they may subsequently sell for extravagant prices if they so wish. However, the current craze around digital art has revealed a hitherto unexplored potential for NFTs. For example, the NFT metaverse connection is undoubtedly an intriguing use of NFTs that deserves additional investigation.

The road to the future of NFTs is paved with various new possibilities for investors, enterprises, and hobbyists, all of which have the potential to impact long-term NFT use and acceptability significantly. Blockchain technology has established itself as one of the most significant technological advancements, rapidly garnering global recognition. Since it served as the foundation for the Bitcoin blockchain, it was essential in resolving the issue of double-spend.

Following that, non-fungible tokens (also known as non-fungible coins) were created using blockchain technology, introducing compatibility and scarcity. However, the rising discussion around NFT metaverse efforts and the growing interest in NFTs and the Metaverse needs more study into the Metaverse's possible role for blockchain and NFTs. Almost every argument about the Metaverse implies the idea of integrating it with non-locality preserving technology (NFTs). Simultaneously, many individuals mistakenly assume that NFTs are merely another component of the larger Metaverse, which is erroneous. Indeed, NFTs and the Metaverse are frequently used interchangeably in the scientific community.

The underlying justification for such an assumption is that the emergence of cryptocurrencies would quickly advance NFTs in blockchain gaming. Virtual worlds will likely be the major medium through which the Metaverse manifests. By delivering services to virtual worlds, interoperable games can help accelerate the emergence of the Metaverse.

Additionally, the connection between genuine identities and digital avatars gives new avenues for establishing access to the Metaverse using non-traditional means. In 2019, a case of NFT-controlled access was demonstrated as the first instance of a metaverse NFT token in use. The inaugural NFT.NYC conference, held in 2019, used an NFT-based ticketing system to admit attendees. Even if no one could refer to the encounter as occurring in the "metaverse," it set a favorable precedent for the NFT's metaverse engagement. In recent years, numerous new efforts have emerged to profit from the confluence of quantum dots and the Metaverse, each of which has a bright future. The programs are mostly focused on fundamentally altering how individuals connect online.

For example, the Decentraland project displays how users may buy real estate within the Metaverse using LAND tokens. The Metaverse is a wide concept, and quantum dots (NFTs) can play a critical role in the larger ecosystem. The creation of Metaverse NFT projects would pave the way for the use of NFTs as a digital property deed. NFTs can be used to get exclusive access to a location in the Metaverse while simultaneously allowing others to gain access to the location. It is worth mentioning that the NFTs' smart contract capabilities might be utilized to enable the selling of

Metaverse real estate. With a few exceptions, the use cases for NFT in the Metaverse would be mostly centered on NFT-controlled access throughout the Metaverse's early stages of development. According to the authors, NFT-controlled access, like the first real-world application of NFTs inside the Metaverse, may assist in securing VIP access to both real-world and Metaverse events.

NFTs are also useful for parachuting branded merchandise or exclusive access to subscribers to a particular channel. Along with boosting fan interaction efficiency, NFTs can provide compatibility outside the Metaverse by developing infrastructure that enables features such as location-based engagement and augmented reality, among others. As a result, the NFTs and Metaverse are co-created.

6.5 NFTs' Effect on the Metaverse

You may have uncovered several ways in which NFTs can contribute to the building of the Metaverse during your search for answers to the question, "Is NFT a component of the metaverse?" However, it is crucial to appreciate the role of NFTs in modifying Metaverse's fundamental architecture. You have probably observed that NFTs have the potential to disrupt traditional social network antecedents in terms of user engagement, transaction, and socializing in the Metaverse. Therefore, how will these ramifications materialize on a greater scale in the Metaverse?

These are some of the most critical components of how the NFT interaction could operate in the Metaverse in the future.

The influence of NFT metaverse programs would also significantly impact the identity, social, and communal experiences of metaverse users. By acquiring NFT assets, people may exhibit their support for a particular initiative or voice their opinions in the digital and real worlds. As a result, like-minded NFT owners may form communities to exchange ideas and collaborate on content creation. The excellent image of NFT avatars exemplifies how the NFT metaverse connection is transforming the world. NFT avatars are composites of the player's genuine self and the imagined self. Players may enter and change between numerous metaverse locations using their own NFT avatars as access tokens.

NFTs may be viewed as an extension of users' real-world identities, providing users with complete ownership, control, and freedom in building virtual identities. By utilizing NFT avatars, users may acquire virtual membership to various experiences in the Metaverse and the real world. As a result, the combination of Metaverse with NFTs has the potential to improve users' social and communal experiences. NFT avatars for company launches and content creation exhibit their potential in the Metaverse.

6.6 NFTs and Metaverse Economy

A typical day in the Metaverse, a widely used immersive virtual world, may resemble our everyday life. We will visit retail malls, travel across the town, meet acquaintances in cafés, and exchange contacts in ways that look stunningly authentic due to substantial advancements in virtual reality and 5G connectivity. Metaverses have been in the framework of multiplayer online games for decades. However, we may soon enter an era in which immersive experiences are indistinguishable from the real world, fostering new forms of interaction for gamers and non-gamers alike.

Decentraland and Somnium Space, two prototype post-production metaverses, already display the beginnings of complete civilization, with humans colonizing land, socializing, trading, and claiming civil freedoms possession. Any civilization must have a functional economy to function properly. The Metaverse economy is based on the authentication of digital commodities, including a person's metaverse home, automobile, farm, books, clothing, furniture, and digital identities.

Additionally, it requires the freedom to travel and trade freely between worlds with varying norms and regulations to prosper. Due to their capacity to validate possessions, property, and even one's own identity, non-fungible tokens – digital records of virtual ownership stored in a blockchain – will serve as the Metaverse's fiscal underpinning. "For them, it all began with the digital art component of NFTs. "It will, however, be far more powerful," Crypto.com Chief Operating Officer Eric Anziani says. In the future, the instrument will be the one that portrays any digital asset in virtual settings". There are several options.

In Decentraland, you will find people speaking by fountains, shopping in fancy boutiques, running along seaside promenades, and users playing different virtual games. Encounters have resulted from the spontaneous formation of real virtual domains by individuals who have purchased land and developed landscapes that have grabbed the imagination of other Decentraland inhabitants. While the experience seems implausible, it is entertaining. Regardless of this, particularly in these early prototypes, the potential is clear and appealing. People gravitate toward fascinating regions in the Metaverse, as in real societies.

Additionally, popularity boosts the value of the virtual property instantly – just like it would be in a real-world area such as Beverly Hills or Paris. The concept of land adjacency is critical for the economy of various metaverses and Decentraland. All metaverse units and the rest of the Metaverse are connected at a fixed location within a defined geography. Additionally, scarcity enables property values to fluctuate, following international economic regulations.

Consequently, as stated in the Decentraland manifesto, a framework for "social knowledge with a financial system fueled by the remaining layers of property ownership and content distribution" is established. This framework is then utilized to carry out the goal of Decentraland. NFTs enable property transfers, which is what powers the Metaverse.

In most cases, these indicators provide more conclusive proof of possession than a property title. Due to how nifty agreements and NFTs are structured, it seems like establishing metaverse property rights in the real world is impossible. "You are aware that you own an asset and can create total ownership." You may then assert ownership rights in that virtual environment based on the environment's conditions and circumstances.

6.7 Identity formation in the Metaverse

Maintaining identity protection is increasingly challenging, especially in well-known physical and online situations. The proliferation of identity management and identity theft protection software demonstrates that digital ambiguity may damage a person's fundamental sense of self in various ways. Securing one's identity has become significantly more difficult with the emergence of increasingly complex metaverses – ranging from familiar internet games to realistic virtual 3D worlds.

As metaverses increasingly resemble the real world – accelerated by the exponential growth of 5G and virtual reality technology – many people's lives will be spent within their intricate domains, both gamers and non-gamers alike. How can we construct a metaverse identity that rapidly evolves from simple pixelated avatars to fully digital twins and alter-egos, complete with all the underpinnings of inner life, in the same way that genetic code establishes biological identity?

One idea is that the solution is found in non-ferrous transitions. Due to the multimillion-dollar transactions involving digital art, memes, and playing cards, these blockchain-based virtual ownership records have spread worldwide. They are now regarded as synonymous with the word "cryptocurrencies." However, the sale of virtual artwork for a world record US$69.3 million in 2021 pales in comparison to the reasons why NFTs are such a big deal.

Their ultimate usefulness is in enabling unambiguous, decentralized ownership of non-physical things such as memes, music, online property, gaming equipment – and, one day, even identity itself – through the provision of unambiguous, decentralized ownership of non-physical assets. A virtual identity can be established similarly to how a virtual concert ticket can be encoded with unique ownership rights and maintained on a blockchain. To be sure, no system or technology can completely safeguard an individual's identity. However, the robustness of blockchain security and the platform fluidity enabled by blockchain decentralization has the potential to dramatically transform the metaverse experience by allowing established identities to wander freely between immersive virtual worlds without being traced.

Chapter 7: The Best Investments in the Metaverse to Skyrocket

By enabling new and unique applications across various sectors, emerging technologies push our established paradigms beyond their original constraints. For instance, it fundamentally altered how people interacted when the internet was introduced. Nowadays, we have internet access virtually wherever we go. After all, the Metaverse asserts that you will be able to interact with and experience the internet as if it were a three-dimensional environment identical to ours in the future. As a consequence of Mark Zuckerberg, Facebook's CEO, renaming the company that controls Facebook to Meta, the discourse over Metaverse's future has accelerated. Numerous metaverse representations have begun to form, each one representing the Metaverse's understanding and viewpoint from the standpoint of the individual.

When it comes to the world around us, the emergence of new technology has accelerated the speed of change. The Metaverse can substantially impact the projects chosen in the blockchain instance. While many believe it will take more than a decade for the Metaverse to materialize effectively, it may occur more swiftly than anybody predicts. Additionally, it is critical to recognize the rising interest in metaverse activities, notably blockchain and cryptocurrency projects. How do cryptocurrency and blockchain technology factor into the Metaverse equation?

Will blockchain-based activities in the Metaverse result in value upgrades for the newly proposed concept of a virtual ecosystem? A thorough assessment of today's most popular metaverse blockchain efforts can give adequate answers to all of these questions. This section summarizes the key blockchain-based projects currently operating in the virtual world. The metaverse notion dominates all discussions about metaverse blockchains and crypto projects. Numerous companies are vying for the right to reserve seats in the Metaverse, with major names such as Facebook, Microsoft, and NVidia leading the effort.

The Metaverse is intended to be a digital ecosystem composed of a collection of distinct virtual worlds, with the metaverse functioning as the primary hub. You may access various services and applications in the Metaverse that act as autonomous sites for various use cases and applications.

Surprisingly, many people assume the Metaverse will not grow shortly. The Metaverse is expanding slowly but steadily. It is still conceivable for new efforts to emerge and collaborate to bridge the divide between various aspects of consumers' digital life. On the other hand, blockchain's critical position in Metaverse's growth marks a good step forward in Metaverse's development.

7.1 The Metaverse's relationship with cryptocurrency

At the moment, most metaverse projects are simply video games that give a three-dimensional experience of the Metaverse. However, numerous other components are necessary for the Metaverse to be constructed. Blockchain technology, more commonly referred to as a cryptocurrency, has the potential to bridge a major gap inside the Metaverse by performing a variety of vital services. The growing number of entries in a list of metaverse crypto projects would demonstrate the Metaverse's enhanced productivity due to blockchain or crypto.

A few of the most prominent blockchain technology or cryptocurrency properties align with the Metaverse's envisioned design.

Proof of Ownership

The blockchain provides digital evidence of possession of assets located inside the Metaverse. It is possible to hold a cryptocurrency wallet, and your private keys may be used to establish your ownership of products or acts recorded on a blockchain. As a result, future Metaverse cryptographic endeavors may benefit from robust and exceptionally secure ways of establishing proof of ownership and digital identification.

Transferring of value

Transferring value is another critical component, another critical feature, in the Metaverse. Additionally, the Metaverse would require a means for transferring value while retaining the trust of its users and other metaverse players. For example, utilizing cryptography on a blockchain is more secure than utilizing in-game cash in multiplayer games. Therefore, users who wish to spend lengthy periods in the virtual world may profit from crypto's trustworthy money.

Compatibility

The finest crypto projects in the Metaverse are also blockchain-based, simplifying collaboration. The blockchain has the potential to enable collaboration across many locations in the Metaverse. For instance, Avalanche and Polkadot enable projects to create blockchains that can communicate with one another.

Governance

Regulations would have to exist in a digital realm that resembles the physical world, and the Metaverse is no exception. Users' primary focus would be establishing rules for interacting with the Metaverse. Blockchain technology provides the ideal platform for transparent and equitable government in the Metaverse, and it may be leveraged to accomplish this.

Collectibles that are one-of-a-kind

The capacity to purchase and sell digital commodities is the most critical feature of Metaverse blockchain-based projects. You need to demonstrate that the assets included within the Metaverse are unique and original concerning the intended real-world occurrences. NFTs enable the creation of unique assets, and blockchain technology may be a useful tool for establishing who owns real objects.

7.2 Top Crypto and Metaverse Projects

When considering Metaverse's blockchain value propositions, it is easy to see why many more crypto projects and metaverse blockchain will emerge. Blockchain technology provides a secure, cost-effective, and transparent method of achieving the Metaverse's primary purpose. With that in mind, let us look at some of the most promising crypto projects and blockchain technologies in the Metaverse.

Decentraland

Decentraland, one of the Metaverse's early pioneers, is essentially a three-3d universe. Players may construct plots of the digital estate in the 3D universe while simultaneously engaging in various other activities. Additionally, players may plan events, socialize with friends, and create unique content on Decentraland.

Indeed, Decentraland has been a well-managed project in the Metaverse for a long period, long before the general public developed a curiosity. The little 2D game, launched in 2016, has grown into one of the most lucrative metaverse crypto businesses, with NFTs now worth hundreds of dollars apiece. MANA, Decentraland's ERC-20 utility token, is available for purchase.

Decentralized crypto initiatives must meet specific criteria in the metaverse cryptocurrency projects, including a 3D interface. Additionally, Decentraland has metaverse-compatible traits, such as in-game activities, a digital marketplace, and components that stimulate social connection with other players. Additionally, Decentraland has achieved extraordinary popularity over the years due to the platform's digital real estate NFT, dubbed LAND, which is accessible for purchase.

Bloktopia

Bloktopia is the second significant addition to the list of leading metaverse blockchain systems and cryptocurrency efforts. It is effectively a metaverse virtual reality game in which you have to navigate around an area that contains a building. The building comprises 21 distinct floors, each representing one of the 21 million Bitcoins currently available in the globe's total quantity. Its primary purpose is to operate as a hub for work, networking, events, and other activities inside the Metaverse. Bloktopia utilizes the Polygon blockchain backed by the Ethereum network for its four key tasks: studying, working and earning, playing, and creating.

Bloktopia's position as one of the leading metaverse blockchain ventures in the modern period is bolstered by the four distinct functions enabled by blockchain. Bloktopia, which uses the native token BLOK, similarly takes a play-to-learn strategy. Additionally, it offers advertising opportunities via Adblock and facilitates real estate transactions via Reblok, among other services. Additionally, several user-created games are accessible, which players may utilize to supplement current content or create entirely new gaming experiences.

Sandbox

The Sandbox is another noteworthy project that has to be featured on our list of the best crypto projects in the Metaverse. It is a blockchain-based metaverse game that allows players to explore a virtual environment through blockchain technology. Users' created environments and other content are included in The Sandbox's virtual universe. The Sandbox has developed into a complex ecosystem that runs on Ether and its currency, SAND. Players may create virtual avatars and identities, which they can link to a wallet address to maintain their NFTs and SAND tokens and a variety of other Ethereum-based assets. With the support of powerful algorithms, gamers may create virtual products and games with unique economic potential like NFTs.

Enjin

Enjin is also a significant inclusion to a list of metaverse crypto initiatives to examine due to its unique properties. It is a blockchain-based framework that enables users to create NFTs as in-game cash. Enjin has successfully released software development kits, more often referred to as SDKs, making it easier to create Ethereum-based NFTs. Enjin commits to providing a secure system for minting NFTs, acknowledging their importance to the Metaverse.

The most eye-catching characteristic of Enjin, one of the top metaverse blockchain ventures, is the liquidity of NFTs. NFTs frequently suffer from illiquidity, which implies that they must be sold before they may be utilized. In contrast, you may swap your Enjin NFT for ENJ tokens to obtain the needed value from your NFT. Additionally, Enjin encourages scarcity and digital collectability, which qualifies it for placement in the Metaverse and the potential to offer liquidity.

Star Atlas

Star Atlas is the Metaverse's greatest and most innovative cryptography project. It is, in essence, a new gaming metaverse built upon the foundations of multiplayer online games, real-time visuals and interactions, decentralized economic institutions, and blockchain technology. Star Atlas's roots on the Solana blockchain demonstrate how it bridges the metaverse and blockchain technology divide, a remarkable accomplishment. Users can purchase digital assets, including equipment, territory, ships, and personnel in the public Star Atlas game metaverse. Star Atlas has an in-game currency system called POLIS, primarily utilized to expedite the game's numerous operations and services. With several unique features and engaging experiences in-store, Star Atlas has a good possibility of quickly ascending to the top of the list of the best metaverse cryptocurrency future projects.

7.3 NFT Games

Many individuals understand the critical nature of digital transformation. If you can read this article in the future, you should be aware of a push to reshape the world through digital transformation. Numerous legacy systems have morphed into novel configurations. NFTs are a frequently employed technological intervention in today's digital transformation arena. They have garnered considerable attention in a relatively short amount of time. Non-fungible tokens, more commonly referred to as NFTs, have extraordinary potential for transforming the gaming industry.

As a result, people are curious about the greatest NFT games and how to select one. The conversation that follows will aid you in understanding more about NFT games and the advantages associated with playing the best NFT games. Additionally, there is a clear picture of the several NFT games that you should instantly begin playing.

How are NFT games defined?

Before delving into the most popular NFT games currently accessible in 2022, it is essential to comprehend what NFT games are. It is essentially a one-of-a-kind blend of traditional gaming elements and novel gameplay methods that the NFT game is all about. The new and growing NFT titles published in 2019 place a premium on giving players more influence over in-game assets. In non-traditional games, players may control in-game assets such as virtual areas, skins, armament, and characters (NFT). To make the concept of NFT games a reality, games must be launched on the blockchain while simultaneously incorporating digital asset-based economics.

Due to their tamper-resistant and one-of-a-kind nature, NFTs are the most often used type of virtual asset in such instances. Additionally, the best NFT games ensure that the NFT token requirements are fulfilled, ensuring the assets' uniqueness and rarity. As a result, the perceived value of blockchain- or NFT-based game assets is frequently higher than the perceived value of other forms of gaming assets.

Players may easily claim control of these assets in games on the NFT games list by utilizing three critical methods combined. Players have the possibility of creating and breeding new characters, earning and unlocking new items, and purchasing digital assets via third-party or local marketplaces. Regardless of how they enter the game, players retain exclusive ownership of the in-game assets they collect while playing. As a result, the NFT games' play-to-earn model is evident, with players able to exchange or sell their various in-game assets.

7.4 Popular NFT games

NFT games provide several benefits over their traditional gaming forebears and some new ones. They changed the gaming business by using blockchain technology, which changed people's perceptions about the worth of in-game items. Players may accumulate extra in-game assets and monetize them in the top NFT games via assets or distribution.

While there are a variety of present and upcoming NFT games to choose from, the most significant disadvantage at the moment would be their quantity. The multiple popular entries in the NFT games world may perplex any newcomer to the universe of NFT games. The following are some of the most well-known names you would expect to see on a list of NFT games in writing.

Infinity Axie

Axie Infinity is a famous NFT game that has grown in popularity over time, and it is one of the most renowned entries in the genre. The game is thematically similar to the Pokémon video game genre, but blockchain technology adds a layer of interest. Axie Infinity's main goal is for players to raise and gather NFT-based animals called Axies, the game's focal point. Axie Infinity, an Ethereum-based game, pits players versus one another in a quest for domination. Players should be aware of Axie Infinity as a unique contribution to the top NFT games. It makes it possible to create a unique genetic identifier for each Axie. As a logical result, players may learn how Axies pass on their defects and strengths to their descendants.

Axies, or digital creatures, are exchanged similarly to any other digital commodity on the Ethereum NFT markets. Before you can start playing the game, you must first gather three Axies, each of which has a different value depending on its distinctiveness and scarcity. Another prominent feature of one of the most well-known NFT gaming is the Smooth Love Potion. It is built on the ERC20 standard and serves as the network's utility token.

Tasks, moving through the adventure mode, and participating in player vs. player combat are all ways for players to gain prizes. SLPs (Smooth Love Potions) may also help players breed young Axies, which can be obtained via trade sites. One of the most notable elements of Axie Infinity is the Axis Infinity Shard, often known as the AXS. It is an ERC-20 token that serves as the platform's governance token and may be used as a native currency on the Axie Infinity platform.

It is an ERC-20 token that serves as the platform's governance token and may be used as a native currency on the Axie Infinity ecosystem.

Gods Unchained

Without a doubt, God's Unchained would be the third game to be added to an NFT games list, if it gets included at all. It is a free-to-play card trading game that incorporates features of NFT into a more classic card trading game environment. Players may acquire cards in various ways, including by purchasing them from other players or by winning them in chance games. Players' card quality and game skills are critical to succeed in Gods Unchained. The intriguing part of Gods Unchained is the proper emphasis on strategies and abilities, which complements the ranked game option.

It is possible to win a battle and earn experience points if your opponent's life is effectively reduced to zero. The experience points you gain will help you advance to the next level, and when the experience meters are full, you will get a new pack of cards. Gods Unchained is widely regarded as one of the greatest NFT games due to the usage of ERC-721 tokens to back up the cards. Alternatively, players may exchange their cards in a native marketplace inside the game or in a public marketplace.

Delta Time F1

Along with the next NFT games, you should watch F1 Delta Time, another fantastic selection. It is similar to a Formula One game in that it allows players to compete in a variety of racing contests using digital currency. Racetracks, cars, drivers, tires, and trinkets are only a few of the game's components. Additionally, it is worth mentioning that souvenirs are available in various racing-grade levels and are created in very limited numbers.

The rarity of marketable commodities in F1 Delta Time is critical to understand in this game. To be more precise, it is one of the few entries on the NFT games list, with many collection categories dependent on their rarity. The four degrees of rarity are as follows: There are four levels of rarity: common, epic, legendary, and apex. The lowest category is Common, followed by Epic, Legendary, and Apex.

Players may acquire collectibles with the native token REVV, and if they own the REVV utility token, they can also use them in tournaments. Additionally, players may resell their REVV tokens on secondary NFT exchanges to earn extra cash. With over $1 million in weekly trading volume and over 1000 new weekly players, F1 Delta Time is one of the most popular NFT games accessible right now.

Splinterlands

Splinterlands would be the last addition to the NFT games that might be played to acquire options. It is just another trading card game similar to God's Unchained. It enables gamers to earn rewards as they browse the game library. To begin the game, players must purchase a pack of cards and then reveal the cards they have obtained during the game. Players who are fortunate enough to acquire rare cards in the opening cards may win larger prizes.

On the other hand, it is probable to locate several similar cards and combine them for increased strength. Once you have mastered the cards, you may duel other players in addition to completing missions. The outcomes of the missions may have a substantial impact on your ability to get various cards.

Chapter 8: Profiting from the Metaverse

Virtual worlds and environments have been popular for a long period. Through games such as The Sims City and the Grand Theft Auto series, people get absorbed in virtual landscapes. Virtual worlds, sometimes referred to as "Metaverse," have been a significant addition to prospective technology due to the games' global popularity.

Metaverses have evolved to the point that many now see them as economically beneficial to the world. Regrettably, before adding this viewpoint, metaverses were virtual instruments with no reality-based basis.

Another topic that has had a considerable influence on the overall state of the economy is blockchain and cryptocurrency. As a result of blockchain's extensive acceptance, the market has been supplied with practical and industrial-based solutions. Consequently, it is projected that digital-based technology would assume the function of providing monetary-based alternatives to the rest of the globe.

The Metaverse as reality is based on science fiction. It is composed of two prefixes: "meta," which means "beyond," and "verse," which means "universal." The Metaverse is the culmination of all internet-enabled digital environments that have been constructed. Virtual and augmented reality technologies have been used to create avatars that converse virtually and hold digital assets that have been end-to-end blockchain secured. It is a virtual-reality environment in which individuals interact with one another in a setting that is generated autonomously.

While metaverses have existed for some time, the underlying technology has not yet enabled the widespread adoption of permissionless credentials, financial sectors, or high-speed exchanges. Rather than that, cryptocurrencies and blockchain technology have built a method for exchanging and storing millions of people's data to create a reality-based link between the virtual and physical worlds.

As metaverses grew increasingly focused on utilizing blockchain technology as a "powerplant" for these platforms, their whole operational idea shifted radically. Metaverses have always had a financial system since they are virtual worlds. Before the advent of blockchain technology in the virtual world, these in-game currencies lacked value due to their lack of physical presence. Soon after blockchain was incorporated into the Metaverse phenomena, the notion of "decentralization" affected the platforms. Blockchain-based platforms have their own NFTs and cryptocurrencies used to generate, manage, and trade virtual assets.

One of the technology's accomplishments was creating true value by allowing for the conversion of NFTs to real currency through Metaverse's specialized NFT markets. Decentraland, Axie Infinity, and SecondLife are all instances of digital environments that have become commercial phenomena, with people earning fortunes due to their participation.

8.1 What is the optimal strategy for investing in metaverses?

As metaverses became standardized as a platform that operated over the blockchain, the public was exposed to various entry kinds. Consequently, investors may invest in the virtual world in both passive and active ways, according to how it operates.

The user is actively engaged in the game and the virtual world. Metaverses are divided into various divisions as a whole universe, each with its own set of uses. A player who plays the game and becomes a member of the Metaverse receives money and NFT tokens. These accumulated tokens have financial value and may be exchanged on any Metaverse's markets. Additionally, users may exchange tokens for various cryptocurrencies.

Users may invest passively in the Metaverse or actively via an active investment approach. The NFT currency, which is used across the Metaverse, or NFT Metaverse, has a monetary value in the crypto realm. As the project increases in size, it may be listed on various exchanges and platforms. Additionally, investors may benefit from pooling their funds across the exchange or platform since it is a member of multiple IDOs and launchpads. This concludes investors' passive involvement in the Metaverse.

Another possible option for investing in Metaverses is for investors to get exposure via purchasing a Metaverse exchange-traded fund (ETF). An ETF is a portfolio of securities and safety nets that trade on the stock market like individual equities. Investors may invest in firms with a significant presence in the crypto ecosystem through a metaverse stock ETF.

8.2 How Can Metaverse Assist You in Earning money?

Participating in the game is one of the most logical methods for the user to earn money in the Metaverse. Due to the "Play-to-Earn" nature of these metaverses, you may earn a large amount of money just by playing the game.

Passive investing is another strategy for profiting from metaverses. Individuals are asked to do due diligence on a project before investing. Identifying the project's exceptional use cases and road map is something that will surely provide you with significant rewards in a short period.

The Metaverse is a tenfold advancement in terms of technology. There is much to offer since these systems are limitless in their capabilities and are capable of performing a wide variety of tasks throughout the virtual world. Since we all accept that the range of metaverses is boundless, several application cases are possible. If you want to reap the benefits of the Metaverse, you must improve your conceptual knowledge. As a result, metaverses will ultimately feature more notions and individuality. Investing in innovation on your own would enable you to increase your profitability significantly.

Virtual worlds and the Metaverse have shown an intuitive technique for connecting the digital and real worlds. Additionally, the Metaverse gives consumers abundant options and reaps enormous advantages from the system.

Conclusion

The inquiry, expansion, and reporting on the Metaverse are accelerating exponentially. Each day, we learn something new. To be a part of the Metaverse, you should monitor these developments closely, preferably daily. Those who do not pursue their education will fall behind.

Bear in mind that innovators such as Bill Gates, Jeff Bezos, and Mark Zuckerberg generate new thoughts.

How are Metaverse, cryptocurrency, and blockchain related? Both the Metaverse and the Blockchain are relatively new concepts. In the Metaverse, blockchain-based gaming is expected to be one of the fastest-growing businesses during the next year. Due to the decentralized nature of blockchain technology, players in metaverse gaming may be able to use a variety of currencies and non-fungible tokens inside the space's virtual landscapes. As a result, Facebook (FB) focuses its efforts on developing a centralized metaverse environment. However, decentralized alternatives are swiftly emerging, with a spate of entrepreneurs attempting to create software that would enable the exchange of digital assets across many blockchains. Cross-transactions across a diverse range of digital assets and tokens are expected to usher in a whole new era of e-commerce in the Metaverse, with some game-focused platforms, such as Decentraland, already seeing rapid growth.

Like art and collectibles, Metaverse books represent a unique use of Metaverse and NFTs. They strengthen client ownership rights, provide extra avenues for authors to market their work, and enable the development of new types of engaging content for prospective clients. However, since metaverse fiction is still in its infancy, the possibilities are limitless. Now is the time for writers to research, experiment, and discover new strategies for promoting and obtaining their works. Even if achieved, the ideas, methods, and powers stated above remain science fiction. In recent years, new advertising strategies have stirred the online world. Certain individuals in the writing and publishing sectors may seem utterly out of control. They should also consider using these new trends to their advantage by doing sufficient research and experimenting with new ideas.

This book is an all-in-one resource for gaining a thorough grasp of the Metaverse. Let us return to the (protracted) history of the World Wide Web. Consider if it was designed to sell adverts or collect user data for commercial gain rather than to facilitate the interchange of research files and discussions between charity and engineers. That is why it is vital to begin the metaverse construction process early.

Suppose these private corporations secure and maintain these platforms as we get into the Metaverse. In that event, they will have far more control over our identities, private conversations, and private data than any previous platform. Investors and organizations alike want to be a part of the next great thing. As a result, interest in the Metaverse is expected to soar. The Metaverse will be a primary focus for Facebook, and it will play a crucial role in the next stage of the internet's growth after the mobile internet.

This is not to say that previous experience or understanding of technology is necessary; the goal is to educate oneself. Adding to your reading list, listening to podcasts, attending online seminars, and purchasing e-courses covering every aspect of the Metaverse are fantastic tools.

Additionally, keep in mind that the Metaverse is arriving quicker than you believe. To be successful in the Metaverse, you must get on the bandwagon first. Develop an understanding of the region of the Metaverse in which you are most interested and make preparations appropriately.

Now that you know what the Metaverse is and how you may invest in it, it is advisable to put the new knowledge you have received from this book to use. You should anticipate investing in stocks, non-fungible tokens, virtual world tokens, and other financial products. Even before the development of NFTs, websites such as Decentraland and The Sandbox enabled anybody to acquire virtual land and even create their settings via technology. The Metaverse is becoming a reality, and as we move closer to that reality, we should anticipate the emergence of further investment opportunities in this space.

Nike has applied for seven trademarks in support of its Metaverse plan. You may want to follow their lead. If you already own a firm or a brand, you may be able to join the Metaverse by simply filing your trademark applications. The same holds for patenting your ideas. To create the ultimate passive cash stream, patent your Metaverse company or financial invention.

When it comes to money, invest as quickly as possible in inequities. Now is an excellent time to buy inexpensive stocks in niche businesses and technology behemoths. The Metaverse's worth will only increase as it takes form. If you are a high-risk trader, tiny technology businesses focused on artificial intelligence are an excellent investment. To ensure your security, invest in well-established companies and diversify your portfolio.

As was the case with Web 2.0, content production will be king in the Metaverse.

When alternatives are few, being one of the first creators will put you on the map. Nowadays, every firm has a digital marketing team in charge of its blogs and social media accounts. On the other hand, large corporations were bewildered in the early days of Web 2.0. Some dismissed Web 2.0 as a youthful fad, while others were too large to make the change quickly. They will be more capable of handling Web 3.0. On the other hand, individuals and small businesses have a great deal of leeway when it comes to adapting to new technologies. One of these individuals may very well be you.

Our journey together has come to an end. You deserve credit for making an effort to learn more about the Metaverse. We wish you well and look forward to seeing you in the Metaverse one day!